FINDING ANSWERS IN
BRITISH ISLES
CENSUS
RECORDS

Try these other great books from Ancestry Publishing

Finding Answers in U.S. Census Records
The Source: A Guidebook to American Genealogy
Finding Your German Ancestors: A Beginner's Guide
Finding Your African-American Ancestors: A Beginner's Guide
Your Swedish Roots: A Step-By-Step Handbook
Finding Your Irish Ancestors: A Beginner's Guide
Finding Your Mexican Ancestors: A Beginner's Guide

FINDING ANSWERS IN

BRITISH ISLES
CENSUS
RECORDS

ECHO KING, AG

ancestry publishing

Library of Congress Cataloging-in-Publication Data

King, Echo.
Finding answers in British Isles census records / by Echo King.
   p. cm.
ISBN 978-1-59331-300-5 (alk. paper)
1. Great Britain—Genealogy—Handbooks, manuals, etc. 2. Great Britain—Census—Handbooks, manuals, etc. I. Title.

CS415.K56 2007
929'.341—dc22

2007009079

Published by
Ancestry Publishing, a The Generations Network™ division
360 West 4800 North
Provo, Utah 84604
www.ancestry.com

First Printing 2007

ISBN-13: 978-1-59331-300-5
ISBN-10: 1-59331-300-4

Printed in the United States of America

Table of Contents

Introduction

What are my ancestors' names? Where were they born? How many children did they have? These are just some of the questions that are answered by the census. While the original purpose of the census was not for family history research, the census is now one of the record types most widely used by people searching for ancestral information.

With millions of names available in census records, how does one find that elusive ancestor? Until recently, the only way for most people to view the census was on microfilm or microfiche. Today the census is available in many forms, from microfilm to digital images on CD or on the Internet. In this book you'll discover how to find your ancestors in the census in all of these forms. You will also learn tips on how to read and interpret the information you find.

Geographic boundaries are changing all the time. The name of a town or county today is not necessarily the same name used 150 years ago. Genealogists most commonly use British places names and boundaries as they existed before the counties were re-organized in 1974 (1975 in Scotland).

As you begin research in the British census, it is important to understand the political divisions in the British Isles region. *Great Britain* refers to the island containing the countries of England, Scotland, and Wales. England, Northern Ireland (since 1922), Scotland, and Wales are officially known as the *United Kingdom*. The Isle of Man and the Channel Islands are crown dependencies and not technically part of the United Kingdom. The term *British Isles* refers to that group of islands found off the northwest coast of Europe. This includes the countries of England, Scotland, Wales, Isle of Man, the Channel Islands, and Ireland (Northern Ireland and the Republic of Ireland).

This book focuses on the censuses taken in Great Britain from 1841 to 1901. In general, however, all statements about the England census apply to the censuses taken in the Channel Islands and the Isle of Man in the same years.

History of the Census in England, Wales, and Scotland

Throughout history, governments and rulers have been interested in knowing all they could about their citizens. A census is one means used by governments to gather statistics and information about large groups of people. Moses, Caesar, and Ghangis Kahn are just a few examples of leaders who have called for a census. Some of the information a census tries to find includes the wealth of the country and the manpower eligible for military service. A current census might even ask how many microwaves one owns. The questions change and evolve over time, but the general intent is the same—for the government to learn about the country's population.

THE ROAD TO CENSUS

Great Britain was slow to adopt the practice of a regular national census compared to other nations. A bill to take an English national census was presented in Parliament as early as 1753, and a numerical census was actually taken in Scotland in 1755. However, opposition to the idea of a census continued for most of the eighteenth century. Some religious-minded individuals argued that a census was sacrilegious and would bring disaster. Others feared that the results would expose any weakness in the country to foreign enemies or simply disliked the idea of the government asking questions about their personal lives.

By the end of the eighteenth century, demand for information was enough to overcome public opposition. Thomas Malthus had recently written his *Essay on the Principle of Population*, which stated that the population of a country might eventually outstrip the country's ability to produce food. Parliament needed information about the population of the country in relation to its ability to produce food. Parliament was also interested the number of men eligible to fight in the ongoing Napoleonic Wars. A census seemed the most pragmatic way to answer these questions.

GREAT BRITAIN GETS A CENSUS

The bill "for taking an Account of the Population of Great Britain and of the Increase or Decrease thereof" passed in the House of Commons in December 1800, and the first official census was taken in March 1801. The census was organized by John Rickman, a secretary for the House of Commons. He assigned the actual census taking to Overseers of the Poor and other local officials in England and Wales, and to schoolmasters in Scotland.

There were only six questions on this first census:

- How many houses are there in the parish, township, or place and how many families occupy them?
- How many people are there in said place, both male and female?
- How many people are employed in agriculture, trade, manufacture, handicraft, or none of those categories?
- What were the number of baptisms and burials in the parish for every tenth year from 1700 to 1780 and then every year from 1781 to 1800?
- What was the number of marriages in the parish or place every year from 1754 to 1800?
- Any comments to add regarding other questions and answers?

The questions were focused on determining the number of people living in the country, the number of people involved in industry and specific occupations, and, somehow, without the benefit of a previous census, whether the population was increasing. Names and other personal details of individuals were not recorded. It must be remembered that the government was more interested in determining how many men of eligible military age were available than in recording details about individuals. The statistics gathered answered the needs of government but are of little use to genealogists.

Following the success of the first census, the government's desire for information overpowered any arguments about privacy for the individual, and a census has been taken every ten years since 1801, with the exception of 1941 when the country was involved with World War II. From 1801 until 1911, Parliament passed a new act for each census. The 1920 Census Act allowed the government to hold a census any time as long as at least five years passed between censuses.

Scotland was included in the census acts for Great Britain from 1801 through 1851 and in 1901 and later. Separate acts of parliament were required in Scotland from 1861 to 1891.

In 1841, the census became a more comprehensive census rather than just a statistical count. This census included detailed questions about individuals' names, ages, occupations, and other personal information, which makes 1841 the first modern census in Great Britain with real genealogical value. The questions on the census, for the most part, remained the same through the nineteenth century (see chapter 7, "Researching Individual Census Years"). In the twentieth century, as the government's need for population information increased, more questions were added. There were about forty questions on the 2001 census of England—quite a change from the six questions in 1801.

The censuses of the Isle of Man and the Channel Islands are covered by the same general statements as those for England and Wales.

To address people's concerns regarding privacy, and to encourage participation, the census records are kept private for one hundred years. Records are not available to the public until the first working day of the 101st year after the census was taken. The 1901 census, made available in 2002, is the most recent census released to the public. The census returns for 1911 will not be available until 2012.

METHODOLOGY OF CENSUS TAKING

As with any record type, one of the first steps to understanding how to use the record is to understand how it was recorded and how it is organized. The census of 1841 was the first census organized and collected through the office of the Registrar General. The organizational system for taking the census has changed very little from the one established in 1841. This system was applied to the censuses of England, Wales, the Channel Islands, and the Isle of Man. In Scotland, the method of taking the census and the arrangement of the census records was very similar to that of England and Wales.

In the early nineteenth century, arranging the census to be taken everywhere at the same time and to be completed in only one or two days was a considerable challenge. However, a simultaneous count seemed to be the best way to prevent omission or double counting.

REGISTRATION DISTRICTS

In 1837, the office of the Registrar General completed the organization of a plan for national civil registration of vital statistics. Under this system all births, marriages, and deaths had be registered with a local registrar. To support this system, England and Wales were divided into over two thousand registration districts. The boundaries to all of these districts were widely published, and officials felt that most people understood the system. It was no surprise that the Registrar General decided to use these same districts as the administrative regions for census taking.

Since civil registration was not introduced in Scotland until 1855, the schoolmasters acted as enumerators from 1801 to 1851. In 1841 and 1851 the schoolmasters were commissioned by the Registrar General in London. After the establishment of civil registration in 1855, the Registrar General for Scotland assumed responsibility for taking the census.

ENUMERATION DISTRICTS

For the census, each registration district was sub-divided into a number of enumeration districts by the local registrar. The ideal size of an enumeration district (ED) was the average number of households the census taker, known as an enumerator, could visit within a single day. Two rough guidelines were that the district should include more than twenty-five households but fewer than two hundred and that the enumerator should not have to cover more than fifteen miles.

Enumeration districts vary in size, depending on the population of an area. In a rural location, a district may cover a large geographic area, but include few people. In towns, the reverse may be true. Consequently, an enumeration district may include either multiple parishes or towns or be a small portion of a larger city.

The 1901 census instructions stated that an enumeration district should not include more than fifteen hundred people, although several thousand enumeration districts exceeded this limit.[1] In addition, institutions such as schools, hospitals, and military barracks with a population of more than two hundred qualified as their own enumeration district.[2] In 1891, the minimum population for institutions as their own enumeration districts was only one hundred.[3]

For the most part, enumeration districts were established in a way that would include a whole parish or town or multiple towns rather than dividing centers of population. If towns or parishes needed to be split, they were supposed to be divided along already existing boundaries, such as townships or wards.[4]

Local registrars were supposed to keep track of population changes in their area over time and adjust the boundaries of enumeration districts to accommodate those changes. However, in some areas changes were not recorded, and you can find enumeration districts in later census years that still use the original boundaries and have unusually large populations. On the other hand, in areas where officials did change boundaries you will find that individuals may not be in the same district census after census, even if they are living in the same house.

ENUMERATORS

The local registrar selected and assigned an enumerator to each enumeration district. In 1851, some of the requested qualifications for an enumerator were:

A person of intelligence and activity; he must read and write well, and have some knowledge of arithmetic: he must not be infirm . . . should not be younger than eighteen years of age, nor older than sixty-five: he must be temperate, orderly, and respectable . . . likely to conduct himself with strict propriety, and to deserve the good-will of the inhabitants of his District.[5]

After viewing the returns, one might argue that skills in writing were not always adequately tested. In some cases, local residents were preferred as enumerators with the hope that they would get greater cooperation from residents. A local enumerator could also fill in some information from personal knowledge. Beginning in 1891, women could qualify as enumerators.

HOUSEHOLDER'S SCHEDULE

The enumerator delivered a questionnaire, called a householder's schedule (see figure 1.1), to each house in the assigned district the week before census day. The enumerator asked each householder to fill out a form and include all individuals who would spend the night in that home on the appointed census night. In the case of institutions, the matron, warden, or other officer in charge was responsible for completing the form.

Printed instructions on each form guided the householder through the census questions about name, age, marital status, relationship, occupation, and mental condition (see figure 1.2). The questions were supposed to apply to everyone who slept in the house on census night, including travelers. Individuals working or traveling during the night were supposed to be enumerated on the schedule at the house where they usually returned in the morning or where they would stop on their journey. Many night workers were missed despite these instructions.

On enumeration day, usually a Monday, the enumerator would return to pick up each household's form. If the form had not been completed, the enumerator was required to complete the form, usually by interviewing someone at the house. In areas where illiteracy rates were high, the enumerator would have spent a great deal of time reviewing and filling in the schedules. Figure 1.3 offers the perspective of a second-time enumerator after he finished his work for the 1861 census.

COPYING, COMPILING, AND COUNTING

After collecting the householder schedules, the enumerator compiled all of the information from the individual schedules into a new book. The Census Enumerators' Books, referred to as CEBs, became the source of information for the clerks at the Register Office. The local registrar was responsible for collecting the CEBs in his district. Once he reviewed the CEBs for accuracy, the registrar bound the CEBs together

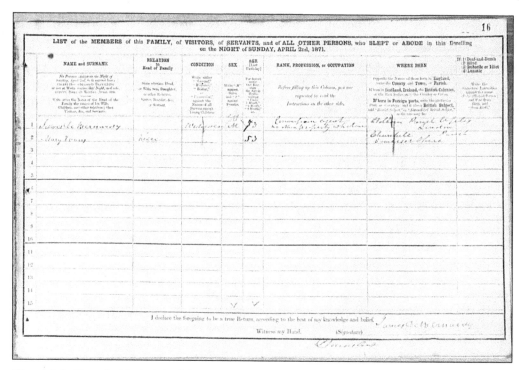

Figure 1.1. Householder's Schedule, 1871, delivered to Hanworth Road, Parish of Isleworth, Middlesex (RG10\1313, f.16).

Figure 1.2. Householder's Schedule Instructional Page, 1871, delivered to Hanworth Road, Parish of Isleworth, Middlesex (RG10\1313, f.16).

into bundles called pieces. Census returns for institutions in the district were usually placed near the end of these pieces. Finally, the local registrar sent all of the pieces to the census office in London where a massive force of clerks processed the statistical information.

Since only the CEBs were required for the government's purpose, most of the original householder schedules were destroyed. Officials did not return the original householder's schedules to London until the 1911 census. Also in 1911, the introduction of punch cards and mechanical sorting replaced the tedious process of compiling statistics by hand. Census officials used computers for the first time in 1961. Today's censuses are almost completely computerized. For more detailed information concerning the methods used to take the census, consult *Making Sense of the Census* by Edward Higgs.

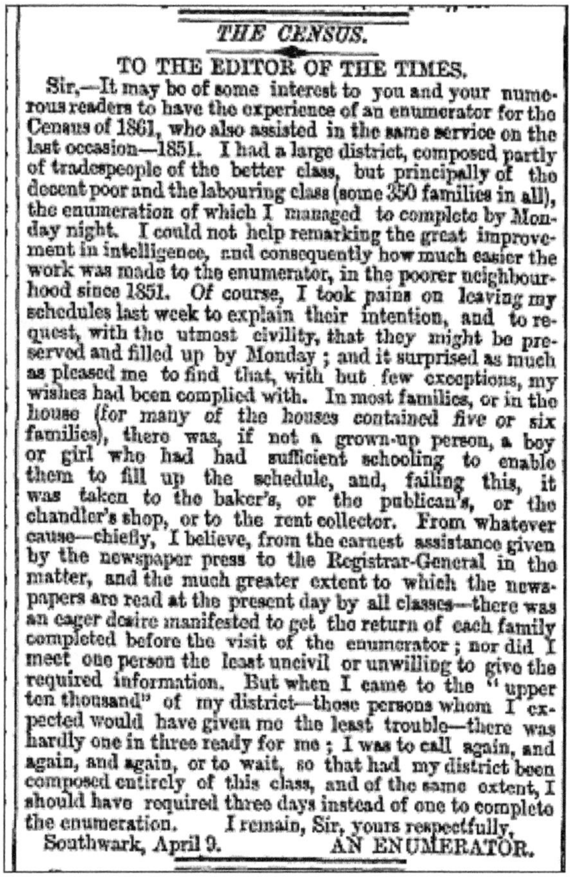

THE CENSUS.

TO THE EDITOR OF THE TIMES.

Sir,—It may be of some interest to you and your numerous readers to have the experience of an enumerator for the Census of 1861, who also assisted in the same service on the last occasion—1851. I had a large district, composed partly of tradespeople of the better class, but principally of the decent poor and the labouring class (some 350 families in all), the enumeration of which I managed to complete by Monday night. I could not help remarking the great improvement in intelligence, and consequently how much easier the work was made to the enumerator, in the poorer neighbourhood since 1851. Of course, I took pains on leaving my schedules last week to explain their intention, and to request, with the utmost civility, that they might be preserved and filled up by Monday; and it surprised as much as pleased me to find that, with but few exceptions, my wishes had been complied with. In most families, or in the house (for many of the houses contained *five or six* families), there was, if not a grown-up person, a boy or girl who had had sufficient schooling to enable them to fill up the schedule, and, failing this, it was taken to the baker's, or the publican's, or the chandler's shop, or to the rent collector. From whatever cause—chiefly, I believe, from the earnest assistance given by the newspaper press to the Registrar-General in the matter, and the much greater extent to which the newspapers are read at the present day by all classes—there was an eager desire manifested to get the return of each family completed before the visit of the enumerator; nor did I meet one person the least uncivil or unwilling to give the required information. But when I came to the "upper ten thousand" of my district—those persons whom I expected would have given me the least trouble—there was hardly one in three ready for me; I was to call again, and again, and again, or to wait, so that had my district been composed entirely of this class, and of the same extent, I should have required three days instead of one to complete the enumeration. I remain, Sir, yours respectfully,

Southwark, April 9. AN ENUMERATOR.

Figure 1.3. Census Enumerator's experience (*The Times* [London], 11 April 1861).

The statistical results compiled from the census were published as Parliamentary Papers. The tables in these papers show numerous statistical results from acreage of each township to water usage and population (see figure 1.4). The tables also show which sub-districts are within a district and the towns and parishes within a sub-district. These tables can be useful for learning more about the size and conditions of a place, as well as what other places are nearby. Places are listed on the tables in roughly the same order as the CEBs were compiled. The published papers also include maps of registration districts by region.

THE CENSUS ON THE WATER

Census collection was a little different for those living onboard ships. In 1841 and 1851, the enumerator totaled up the number of individuals living onboard canal boats and added that number to the totals for that enumeration district. In 1851, ships in port or in British waters were treated like institutions and enumerated separately. Crews of ships at sea or in foreign ports were not counted in 1841 and 1851. Starting in 1861, special shipping schedules were used to account for all British vessels anywhere at sea (see figures 1.5 and 1.6).

| 16 | | 22 GLOUCESTERSHIRE.—PARISHES. AREA; HOUSES, 1841, 1851; | | | | | | | | | | | | | | | [Div. VI. |

No. of District.	No. of Subdist.	DISTRICT or UNION. / SUBDISTRICT.	No. of Parish	Parish, Township, or Place.	Area in Statute Acres.	HOUSES 1841 Inhabited	1841 Uninhabited	1841 Building	HOUSES 1851 Inhabited	1851 Uninhabited	1851 Building	POPULATION. PERSONS. 1801	1811	1821	1831	1841	1851
		329 BRISTOL.‡															
		BRISTOL—															
329	1	ST.MARY REDCLIFF	1	St. Mary Redcliff - Parish		1166	47	3	1079	62	5	4131	4696	5827	6259	7025	6812
			2	Temple - - - Parish		981	76	9	928	42	2	3716	4690	5343	5981	6189	6060
			3	St. Thomas - - Parish		194	32	5	200	30	-	1195	1294	1276	1361	1403	1508
	2	CASTLE PRECINCTS	1	St. Nicholas - Parish		239	20	-	272	6	-	1849	1819	1892	1916	2166	2076
			2	St. Stephen - a Parish		235	18	-	208	9	-	1761	1671	2078	1278	2269	2778
			3	St. Leonard - b Parish		42	11	-	23	20	1	285	329	265	302	281	123
			4	St. Werburgh - Parish		22	8	-	17	27	1	146	144	116	100	99	99
			5	All Saints - Parish		34	13	-	29	11	-	182	150	173	180	174	154
			6	St. Ewin - Parish		10	4	-	9	3	-	117	103	99	74	55	52
			7	St. John - Parish		147	4	-	147	26	-	700	704	757	889	938	1190
			8	Christchurch - Parish	1840	147	28	-	136	31	-	690	894	1029	1193	1092	1079
			9	St. Mary-le-Port - Parish		37	15	-	38	16	-	289	288	302	247	277	230
			10	St Peter - c Parish		193	22	-	187	11	4	1566	1546	1623	1776	1545	1470
			11	Castle Precincts Extra Par.		280	16	11	279	23	-	1404	1535	1526	1804	1830	1825
	3	ST. PAUL	1	St. Philip and Jacob d In-Par.		658	39	-	676	59	-	2355	2834	3673	3886	4110	4521
			2	St. Paul - e In-Parish		1631	58	7	1645	122	1	4958	6056	7320	9146	10762	10758
	4	ST. JAMES	1	St. James - f In-Parish		1437	126	6	1411	146		7307	8241	8804	10488	10555	10658
	5	ST. AUGUSTINE	1	St. Michael - g Parish		625	25	1	625	46	-	2786	3103	3445	3836	4254	4431
			2	St. Augustine-the-Less h Parish		1198	49	5	1213	101	1	5377	6495	7321	8358	9242	9891
		330 CLIFTON.															
330	1	CLIFTON	1	Clifton - - - i Parish	740	1907	80	67	2498	162	41	4457	6981	8811	12032	14177	17634
	2	ASHLEY	1	St. James and St. Paul - k United Out-Par	490	1130	85	16	1408	79	30	1897	2427	3605	4495	6139	7935
			2	Horfield - l Parish	1287	121	5	-	160	4	-	119	146	198	328	620	998
				Military in Horfield Barracks		-	-	-	-	-	-	-	-	-	-	-	223
	3	ST. GEORGE	1	St. George - m Parish	1831	1603	92	14	1768	125	5	4028	4909	5334	6285	8318	8905
	4	ST. PHILIP AND JACOB	1	St. Philip and Jacob n Out-Parish	310	3543	185	60	4215	432	67	8406	10702	11824	15777	21590	24961
	5	WESTBURY		*Westbury-upon-Trym* Parish—*													
			1	Westbury-upon-Trym -		322	25	2	349	8	5	678	957	1203	1515	1707	1883
			2	Stoke Bishop - o Tything	5456w	447	42	13	658	26	19	1293	q1588	1883	2328	2651	4213
			3	Shirehampton - p Tything		131	7	-	134	4	-	354	490	635	420	671	632
				Henbury, part of Parish—† q													
			4	Kings Weston - Tything		31	-	-	28	-	-	154		154	107	184	207
			5	Lawrence Weston - Tything		64	-	-	66	-	-	247	744	335	329	341	334
			6	Henbury - Tything		86	2	-	88	4	-	437	447	431	390	442	434
			7	Stowick - Tything	9892w	102	3	2	104	2	-	323	403	467	568	552	526
			8	Compton - Tything		26	-	-	26	-	-	151	-	151	159	144	141
			9	Charlton - Tything		75	2	-	88	1	-	99	186	296	310	329	411
			10	Compton Greenfield - Parish	650	8	-	-	10	-	-	24	35	42	40	65	64
	6	STAPLETON	1	Filton - Parish	1030	56	-	-	54	6	-	115	168	210	217	276	245
			2	Stapleton (w) (w) r Parish	2554	628	35	2	709	29	2	1541	1921	2137	2715	3944	4840
			3	Stoke Gifford - Parish	2065	90	-	-	95	2	-	281	315	376	441	480	488
				Winterbourne Parish—‡													
			4	Winterbourne - s -		425	35	9	333	42	-	1592	1569	1659	1939	1950	1430
			5	Frenchay and Hambrook - Tything	3170	242	12	3	319	4	-	1592	764	968	950	1201	1446
		331 CHIPPING SODBURY.															
331	1	CHIPPING SODBURY	1	Westerleigh - t Parish	4009	358	12	-	347	5	-	1582	1632	1817	1709	1776	1679
			2	Pucklechurch - u Parish	2428	177	12	1	189	4	-	542	535	612	796	862	931
			3	Wapley-cum-Codrington Parish	2448	68	-	-	68	-	-	258	276	307	253	366	305
			4	Chipping Sodbury - u Parish	120	285	14	1	253	22	-	1090	1235	1059	1306	1273	1195
			5	Old Sodbury - u Parish	3637	182	1	1	161	2	-	687	765	803	729	871	820
			6	Dodington - Parish	1473	19	-	1	22	1	-	95	113	106	113	143	135
	2	MARSHFIELD	1	Dirham and Hinton - Parish	3005	100	-	-	96	3	-	437	476	526	516	530	474
			2	Wick and Abson - x Parish	2315	171	9	1	179	4	1	571	671	715	824	794	816
			3	Doynton - Parish	1703	91	4	-	91	2	-	303	342	415	448	529	499
			4	Cold Ashton - y Parish	2300	86	4	-	93	4	1	224	268	284	322	414	479
			5	Marshfield - z Parish	5845	334	3	1	365	12	4	1246	1415	1569	1651	1674	1648
			6	West Littleton - Parish	1009	29	1	-	23	1	-	100	88	109	128	158	161
		Entire Parishes of															
				* Westbury-upon-Trym - - - -	5456w	900	74	15	1141	38	24	2325	3035	3721	4263	5029	6728
				† Henbury - - - - -	15409w	470	10	2	490	11	-	1688	2134	2283	2351	2439	2525
				‡ Winterbourne - - - -	3170	667	47	12	652	46	-	1592	2333	2627	2889	3151	2876

NOTE—The letter (w) inserted after the name of a Parish or place denotes that a Workhouse is included in the Return; (w) indicates that the Return includes a Workhouse not belonging to the Union or District in which it is situate. Union Workhouses under the New Poor Law have been established since the Census of 1831. The names of places printed in capitals, thus—(DURSLEY)—are those of Parishes which contain Towns of the same name; Cities and Boroughs are distinguished in the same manner. When a Parish or place is not in the County named at the head of the page, the County to which it belongs is stated in *italics*. The AREAS printed in Arabic figures, thus—(490, St. James and St. Paul)—are those assigned to the Parishes and places by the late Mr. Rickman, in the Enumeration Abstract of 1831; in these cases the records in the custody of the Tithe Commissioners do not supply Major Dawson with the means of arriving at a more accurate result. The Areas distinguished thus (w) include Water or Sea-coast.

Figure 1.4. Population Table 1851 (*Population Tables I: Numbers of Inhabitants: 1852–53* (1631–1632), LXXXV, 1, p.16).

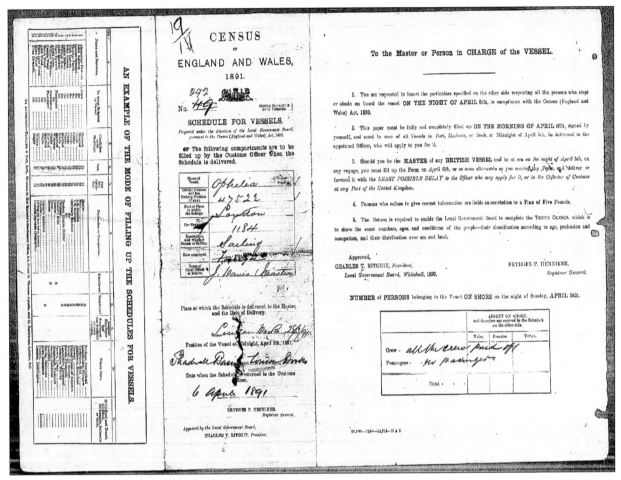

Figure 1.5. Title page for ship *Ophelia* in 1891 (RG12\291, f.55).

NOTES

1. Edward J. Higgs, *Making Sense of the Census: The Manuscript Returns for England and Wales, 1801–1901* (London: Her Majesty's Stationary Office, 1989), 38.

2. Office of Population, *Report on 1851 Census, Great Britain: Including Population Tables, 1801–1851* (London: Her Majesty's Stationary Office, 1852), xii.

3. Higgs, *Making Sense of the Census,* 38.

4. Office of Population, *Report on 1851 Census,* cxxxv.

5. Office of Population, *Report on 1851 Census,* cxxxv.

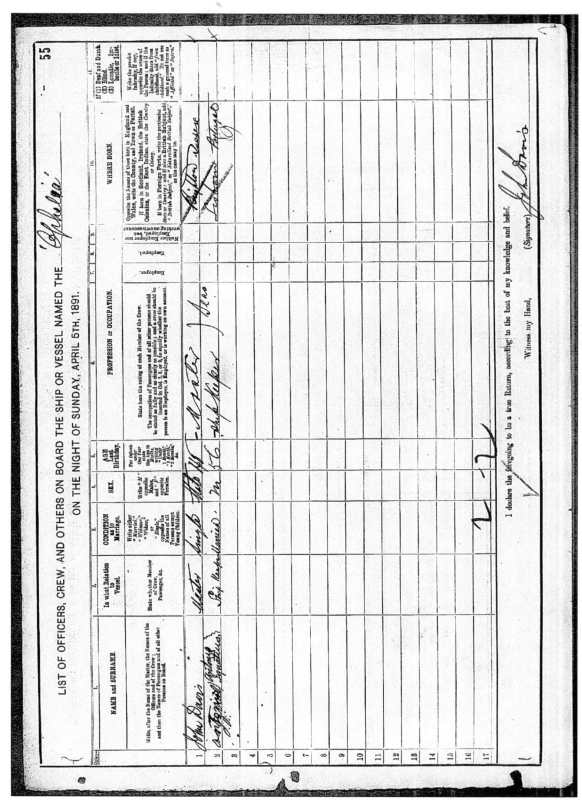

Figure 1.6. Completed census schedule for ship *Ophelia* (RG12\291, f.55).

2

Understanding the Census

The census is one of the most used record groups in family history research. Unlike other records that show a single event for two or three certain people at any given time, the census is a picture of the entire population taken at one point in time. This "snapshot" of history is like opening a window into the lives of our ancestors as it shows us where they lived, with whom they associated, and what they were doing with their lives.

From the census, we get a picture of what entire households looked like. In all but the 1841 census, we even get specific relationships. This not only helps us put family groups together, it can also help us place individuals in a certain location at a specific time. The census can also place individuals and families at various locations at times in life prior to the census. For instance, discover where and when an ancestor was born or track a family's movement by the birthplaces and approximate birth dates of children. Information from the 1841 census can take you back into the late eighteenth century. Census returns include other information, such as language spoken, occupation, or housing situation. Few, if any, other records can provide such a wide range of information. Census records are some of the most detail-rich and interesting records available.

Details in the census may lead you to other record sources beyond the census, including probate records, immigration records, military records, or apprentice records. The second biggest record group used in research in England and Wales is civil registration. Since the census uses the same administrative regions as civil registration, there is a direct link between the two record types. Use the registration district listed on a birth certificate to get started in the census, or use the registration district where you locate an individual in the census as a clue of where to find the correct birth or marriage certificate.

Although the census is a very valuable source, we should not forget that every source has certain flaws. Understanding how the records were created and what problems occurred at that time helps us understand and work around the weak points in the census.

People make mistakes, whether intentional or not. One of the most likely times for errors to occur is when a copy is made. As mentioned in the previous chapter, enumerators made copies of the household schedules they collected. The data that you see when you view a page from the census, whether it is digital, microfilm, microfiche, or even the original paper documents, is already at least one copy away from the information reported by your ancestors. Some of the more common copy errors include people who were skipped or added as well as simple transcription errors.

MISSING OR ADDITIONAL RECORDS

One might easily assume that everyone in the country was counted in the census. In reality it would be impossible to find and count every single person. Some individuals were traveling, either out of the country or within the country, and not at an enumerated establishment. Others chose to avoid the census taker for personal reasons. Enumerators simply missed others in the crowded areas of large cities. The following letter to the editor describes a situation where a householder's schedule was missed:

> Sir, I live in a large house in a broad and very lengthy street in the [South West] district, and in the mansion I and my family and servants inhabit there are five sets of apartments, each occupied by families, numbering several persons, young and old, and their domestics. Observing in *The Times* of to-day a letter from a gentleman in Peckham that his census paper had not been called for, it occurred to me to inquire about the fate of the similar document, which, fully and carefully filled in according to direction endorsed thereon, I had given to my butler on Monday morning early for the collector or enumerator who was to call for it, and I was informed that no one up to present time had been for it (it is now noon April 3); and I have moreover ascertained that there has not been the least evidence of any inquiry having been addressed to the families who are handier to the Census Office then Peckham, and who have more than 200 ft of frontage in one of the chief streets of western London. I have written to report as requested to the Registrar-General's Office, Millbank, but to make assurance doubly sure, I also write to *The Times*.[1]

As many as five families were possibly missed according to this account.

LOCATING "MISSING" INDIVIDUALS

Sometimes there is an assumption that a family has been missed because they do not appear "in order" on the returns. Before assuming this, examine the facts to make sure you understand how the returns are ordered. Enumerators did not carry the Census Enumerators' Book with them and they did not always copy the entries into their books in order by address. In some cases, it appears that the enumerator tried to arrange the families in his district so that they fit neatly onto a page rather than keeping them in any certain order. You may need to examine an entire district if families are not listed according to street address.

An enumerator did not always cover both sides of the street. The other side of the street might not be in the enumeration district you are looking in. If an enumerator did canvass both sides of the street, it is unlikely that he crossed back and forth across the street to get each house. Most enumerators were more likely to walk down one side of the street and then turn at the end of the street to come back up the other side in the shortest route possible. If the house numbers seem to be all even or all odd, this is the possible case.

Figure 2.1 shows a map drawn on the description page for one enumerator's district. The map shows that only parts of certain streets were included.

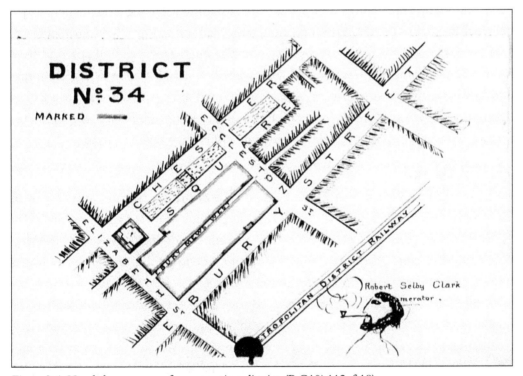

Figure 2.1. Hand drawn map of enumeration district (RG10\112, f.19).

Even in cases where the families are listed by street, consider that streets could be called by different names at different times. Parts of a street may appear as named terraces, cottages, or courts. House numbers were often erratic; they might not have even been in sequential order on the street, and they may even be duplicated. Review the entire street if you do not find a family at the address you expected to.

There are many other reasons why you do not find individuals where you expect them. They may be listed with a name other than the one you expect. If an ancestor remarried, you may find children listed under a new surname. If you are using an index, the name may have been transcribed incorrectly. Your ancestor may not have been present on census night. Families may have moved, and you may need to use additional resources to locate a new address. Exhaust all possibilities before presuming an individual or family was skipped by the enumerator.

DUPLICATE AND FALSE ENTRIES

On occasion, you may find duplicate entries for an individual, although missing or skipped names are more common. If an individual visited two different households on census night, you may find him or her recorded in both places. Travelers or night laborers are sometimes recorded in multiple locations.

On rare occasions the enumerator may have added false entries. The work was difficult, and many enumerators completed their assignment feeling inadequately compensated (see figure 2.2). At least one enumerator filed suit against the Home Secretary after completing his work on the 1851 census. The enumerator was supposed to have been paid 18 shillings for the first 300 names and 1 shilling for every 60 over the first 300. He had counted only 50 extra people and wanted to be paid the appropriate fraction of the fee for 60 additional people.[2] It is not hard to imagine that some enumerators would simply add in ten additional people rather than take the issue to court.

LOST INFORMATION

Even if individuals were properly enumerated, some of the information may have been lost over the years. This could be due to age and general wear and tear, copy errors by the enumerator, or skipped pages when the microfilm or digital copy was made. Pages skipped during filming or digitizing can sometimes be located in the originals. If you suspect that a page is missing, check the folio numbers.

Although all of the schedules have printed page numbers on them, all of the returns for England and Wales were stamped with a folio number before they were filmed. A folio number appears in the top right corner on the front side of each schedule and refers to both the front page and the back page of that schedule. One way to check to see if a page is missing is to make sure that all of the folios are there. If one side of the folio appears to be missing, a page may have been missed when it was microfilmed or

THE CENSUS ENUMERATORS.—The enumerators employed in taking the late Census, especially those in the more thickly-populated districts, are loud in their expressions of dissatisfaction at the small amount of remuneration which has been fixed by the Government for their services, and within the last few days several meetings have been held in the east and north-east of London with the view of taking measures to induce the Government to make some addition to the proposed rate of payment. At the last of these it was stated that the labour of the enumerators engaged in taking the Census of 1871 was much greater than at the preceding Census, nearly double the amount of writing being required in copying the returns, while the remuneration now offered is precisely the same as that paid ten years since, viz.:—A sovereign for the first 400 entries, each entry comprising on an average about eight words, and and 2s. 6d. per 100 for every 100 afterwards. It was stated that the work which had been performed was not only difficult in many cases, but not altogether free from danger, an enumerator present having caught smallpox while discharging his duties. One speaker stated that he had made an estimate of the time he was employed, and found that for this exceptional work, for which he submitted Government should pay liberally, he would receive, according to the proposed rate of payment, something like 4d. an hour. After considerable discussion it was ultimately determined that a memorial should be transmitted to Mr. Alderman Lusk, who had undertaken to present it to the Home Secretary, and a deputation was appointed to wait upon the right hon. gentleman to urge the subject upon his consideration.

Figure 2.2. Census Enumerators' experiences (*The Times* [London], 20 May 1871).

digitized. You can contact The National Archives in Kew, England, to see if it is possible to check the original manuscript or have it checked for you. If the printed page numbers are out of sequence, but the folio numbers are in sequence, the page is most likely missing from the originals and cannot be replaced.

CLERICAL ERRORS

Enumerators had the tedious task of copying poorly written responses from householder schedules or copying their own notes taken from verbal responses. Many factors can influence the quality of the resulting copy. Enumerators struggled to read poor handwriting, just as we do today, and some made mistakes in the process. If a person gave a verbal response, the enumerator may have misheard it and in turn spelled it wrong.

The copy process is prone to errors. As mentioned above, some people that may have been recorded correctly on the householder's schedule were dropped in the copy made by the enumerator. In some cases, the forms themselves led to errors. For example, on the householder's schedule there were two separate columns for *gender* and *age*. The Census Enumerator's Book has two columns as well; however, one is for *male age* and one is for *female age*. It is not unusual to find individuals whose gender is recorded incorrectly in the CEB.

As a researcher, you need to use some creativity to locate phonetically spelled place or personal names. Literacy rates were low, and spelling standards were not rigid. Local accents have some influence on how a name may have been pronounced or understood. For example, a place name that begins with a vowel may written as if it started with an "H." On the other hand, a place name that starts with an "H" followed by a vowel may be recorded as though the name began with a vowel and without the "H."

MISLEADING ANSWERS

Even when the information is clear and legible, not all answers are exactly accurate. Some individuals purposely gave misleading answers or no answers at all. Members of the poorer population, especially older individuals, may have lied about their birthplace out of fear of being returned to their original parish under the Poor Law.

Others may have given the best response they could and still have been less than accurate. A person may have moved into a parish when he was small and given that place as his birth location, not knowing the truth to be any different. Even today, it is common practice for people to say they were born in the nearest large town rather than a smaller town or village. Since you do not know the circumstances, verify all information against another source when possible.

As with birthplace, individuals may have been ignorant of their exact age or reluctant to divulge such personal information. In fact, it is quite possible to find people who have aged only a few years since the previous census according to their answers. People are notorious for fudging on that detail of their lives.

In a letter to the editor of *The Times,* one woman expressed her concern about stating her age:

> There are thousands of both sexes who will bear me out in saying that as
> we advance in years the necessity of putting down our age in the Census

paper becomes a trying thing. Our neighbors probably know our age approximately, but that is different from writing down the exact number of years for them all to scan at their pleasure. . . . While the mind is slightly calmed by the assurances in the newspapers that the enumerator is bound to secrecy, and that the disagreeable fact will be at once sent away to a distant collector.

Vain delusion! This very day I discovered that, instead of the Census papers being delivered on the Monday evening last to the collector for the district, all those belonging to this parish still lie in a drawer in the enumerator's house, and on calling there this afternoon I was even invited to look at them . . . the good lady of the house had no idea the papers were not intended for the public gaze.[3]

A fine was levied against those who lied or refused to cooperate, but some people would rather pay the fine than give out their personal information. In 1891, one Mr. J. Morgan appeared before the superintendent registrar of his district for failing to complete the form left at his house. On the householder's schedule, he had entered "Myself, my wife, and three children slept under the roof of this house on April 5. All other questions are of an inquisitorial nature and I absolutely refuse to answer any of them or allow any one in my house to do so." At the conclusion of the session with the superintendent registrar, Mr. Morgan had been persuaded to complete the form. However, he also went to prison for seven days rather than pay the fine to complete his punishment.[4] Looking at the CEB from this district, it appears that the enumerator squeezed that additional information provided by Mr. Morgan into the CEB that had been completed prior to Mr. Morgan's hearing (see figure 2.3).

In institutions, the warden or other head official was responsible for completing the form. In many cases, the residents of hospitals, asylums, and homes for the aged were unable to provide personal information, and the staff may not have been able to answer for them. In some institutions, limited information was entered either to protect privacy or to save time.

GEOGRAPHY AND BOUNDARIES

Understanding the relationships between places and the various ecclesiastical and civil jurisdictions in the British Isles can be a bit of an obstacle, especially for researchers who are not native to the area. Familiarity with good maps and gazetteers is essential for thorough research.

The main geographic divisions used by researchers of the census are county, civil parish, ecclesiastical parish, and registration districts.

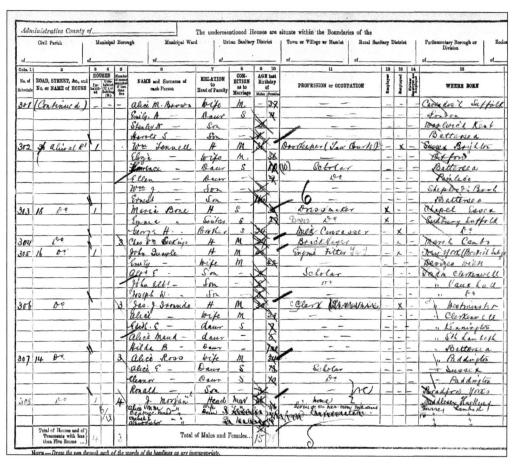

Figure 2.3. Census return for J. Morgan, 1891 (bottom three lines) (RG12\436, f.82, p.42).

COUNTIES

The county names used in the 1841–1901 censuses were those in existence before the changes made to the size and names of some counties in 1974 in England and Wales and in 1975 in Scotland. Maps of the counties both before and after the re-organization are available at <www.familysearch.org>.

There are fifty-one ancient counties in England and Wales. The one major change to what are called the ancient counties was in 1889 when the administrative county of London was created from the City of London and parts of Middlesex, Kent, and Surrey. Family historians often use a list of three letter codes, known as the Chapman County Codes, when referencing these counties (see table 2.1).

PARISHES

A parish is a geographic unit used as the basis for many census indexes and finding aids. In Scotland, the parish is the fundamental administrative organization. To see where a parish is located within a county, or relationships between parishes, consult

Table 2.1: Chapman County Codes for Pre-1974 Counties

CHANNEL ISLANDS (CHI SOMETIMES JUST CI)

ALD	Alderney
GSY	Guernsey
JSY	Jersey
SRK	Sark

ENGLAND (ENG)

BDF	Bedfordshire		LIN	Lincolnshire
BRK	Berkshire		LND	London (since 1889)
BKM	Buckinghamshire		MDX	Middlesex
CAM	Cambridgeshire		NBL	Northumberland
CHS	Cheshire		NFK	Norfolk
CON	Cornwall		NTH	Northamptonshire
CUL	Cumberland		NTT	Nottinghamshire
DBY	Derbyshire		OXF	Oxfordshire
DEV	Devon		RUT	Rutland
DOR	Dorset		SAL	Shropshire
DUR	County Durham		SOM	Somerset
ESS	Essex		SFK	Suffolk
GLS	Gloucestershire		SRY	Surrey
HAM	Hampshire		SSX	Sussex
HEF	Herefordshire		WAR	Warwickshire
HRT	Hertfordshire		WES	Westmorland
HUN	Huntingdonshire		WIL	Wiltshire
KEN	Kent		WOR	Worcestershire
LAN	Lancashire		YKS	Yorkshire
LEI	Leicestershire			

ISLE OF MAN (IOM)

SCOTLAND (SCT)

ABD	Aberdeenshire		BAN	Banffshire
ANS	Angus		BEW	Berwickshire
ARL	Argyllshire		BUT	Buteshire
AYR	Ayrshire		CAI	Caithness

Table 2.1: Continued

CEN	Central		NAI	Nairnshire
CLK	Clackmannanshire		OKI	Orkney Islands
DFS	Dumfries-shire		PEE	Peebles-shire
DNB	Dunbartonshire		PER	Perthshire
ELN	East Lothian		RFW	Renfrewshire
FIF	Fife		ROC	Ross and Cromarty
INV	Inverness-shire		ROX	Roxburghshire
KCD	Kincardineshire		SEL	Selkirkshire
KRS	Kinross-shire		SHI	Shetland Islands
KKD	Kirkcudbrightshire		STI	Stirlingshire
LKS	Lanarkshire		SUT	Sutherland
MLN	Midlothian		WLN	West Lothian
MOR	Morayshire		WIG	Wigtownshire

WALES (WAL)

AGY	Anglesey		GLA	Glamorgan
BRE	Breconshire		MER	Merionethshire
CAE	Caernarvonshire		MON	Monmouthshire
CGN	Cardiganshire		MGY	Montgomeryshire
CMN	Carmarthenshire		PEM	Pembrokeshire
DEN	Denbighshire		RAD	Radnorshire
FLN	Flintshire			

a good map, such as Cecil Humphrey-Smith's *The Phillimore Atlas and Index of Parish Registers.*

In England and Wales, the most common place of residence in the census is the civil parish. Civil parishes are relatively new and have grown out of the older administrative units of ecclesiastical parish and township. In 1889, guidelines established a civil parish as the lowest level of local civil government.

In southern England, townships and ecclesiastical parishes tend to exist within the same boundaries, while northern parishes tend to cover multiple townships. In the nineteenth century, townships became known as civil parishes as they took on functions of poor relief and other duties formerly administered by the church parishes or townships. Consequently, in the south, the boundaries of ecclesiastical parish and civil parish often coincide, while in the north an ecclesiastical parish may cover many civil parishes.[5] You can determine to which civil parish a town or small place belongs by consulting a good gazetteer.

In Scotland, each parish is assigned a unique number. This parish or district number is often used to reference a particular place in source citations and is often required when using indexes or reference materials. The numbering begins in the north of the country and moves south from east to west. Within each county, the parishes are arranged alphabetically and then numbered consecutively. In 1854, when new registration districts were created, the new districts were provided with a new sequence of numbers. The parish number used in the census will correspond to the parish number used in church records. A list of these numbers can be obtained from the General Register Office for Scotland <www.gro-scotland.gov.uk> (and in appendix B).

REGISTRATION DISTRICTS

When the civil registration system was created in England and Wales, the country was divided into eleven regions and then subdivided into Superintendent Registrar's Districts based on the old Poor Law Unions. These registration districts were then subdivided again into sub-districts. Registration districts are administrative areas and can overlap geographic county lines. Since the census was taken according to registration district, you may find neighbors in the same parish and enumeration district but living in two different counties. When Scotland was divided into registration districts, the district boundaries corresponded to parish boundaries, making it possible to have a census return for each parish. Maps of registration district boundaries can be found in the Population Tables or on maps created by and available for purchase from the Institute of Heraldic and Genealogical Studies <www.ihgs.ac.uk>. An incomplete set of maps is also available at The National Archives in Kew.

SEARCH ACROSS BOUNDARIES

All of this demonstrates that boundaries exist only on maps and for administrators. We cannot limit ourselves geographically. A single town could reside in one registration district but in two counties. Alternatively, it could exist in one county, but in multiple registration districts, as was the case in London. As you search the census, keep the geography of the place in mind. It is helpful to have a map close by. While a possible match for an ancestor found a hundred miles away from where expected might not be the most likely match, it is not completely impossible.

LEGIBILITY

Perhaps one of the biggest challenges with the census is reading the handwriting. Old handwriting can be hard to read and it is even worse when clerks have marked through the very information you are trying to read. A researcher can overcome the challenge of reading older handwriting by taking some time to become familiar with the scribe and by practicing the skill.

Take time to become familiar with the handwriting of a particular enumerator by reading a few pages before and after the page you are trying to decipher. Look for familiar words, such as the names of counties or relationships, and see how the letters are formed. Try building an alphabet by copying readable letters and comparing them to letters that are hard to read. When trying to decipher ages, use numbers that run in sequence, like household numbers, to help you determine unreadable numbers.

If the previous methods do not work, you can try to sound the word out, remembering that accents vary from place to place. Sometimes it helps to get a fresh look. Take a break and then come back and give it another try, or try looking at it from another angle. Tables 2.2 and 2.3 may be helpful as you sound out and decipher letters. Sometimes another person will have more success. If you are viewing a digital image, you can manipulate the image in different ways to make it more readable. For example, you may be able to adjust brightness and contrast or view the image as a negative.

NOTES

1. Quis Custodiet?, "Census Returns," The Times [London], 4 April 1901, 6.
2. "Cohen Exparte v. Sir George Grey, Bart.—The Census Enumerator and the Home Secretary," Daily News [London], 28 May 1851, 6.
3. An Old Maid of A Certain Age, "The Census," The Times [London], 8 April 1871, 8.
4. "Police," The Times [London], 20 April 1891, 13.
5. Mark D. Herber, Ancestral Trails: The Complete Guide to British Genealogy and Family History (Baltimore: Genealogical Publishing Company, 1998), 89.

Table 2.2: Phonetic *and* Misread Letters

a	e, i, o, u, y, ey, eh
au	ow, ou
b	p, v, bb, pp
bb	b, p, pp
c (as in *catch*)	k, g, gh, q, cc, ck
c (as in *chin*)	ch, cz, s, sh, tch, tsh, z, dg
ch	c, k, g, gh, sh, h (as in *Chanukah*), ju (as in *San Juan*)
chr	kr, gr, cr
ck	k, c, g, q
cr	kr, chr, gr
cz	c, ch, ts, lz, s, sh, tcr, tsh
d	dd, t, dt
dd	d, t, tt
dg (as in *dodge*)	g, j, ch, gg, tj
ds (as in *bends*)	z, ts
dt	d, t, tt
e	a, ee, i, o, u, y, ie, ea
ea	e, i, y, ie, ei
eau (as in *beau*)	o, aw, ow, au, ou
ee	ie, e, i, y, ea, ei
ew	u, oo, ou
f	v, ph, pf, gh, il (as in *calf*), ff
ff	f, ph, gh, v, lf (as in *calf*)
g	c, ch, gg, gh, j, k, q, dg, h (as in *Gila Monster*)
gg	g, ch, k, q, j
gh (as in *ghost*)	c, ch, g, gg, ch, k, q
gh (as in *laugh*)	f, ph, pf, v, lf
gn (as in *gnat*)	n, kn
gr	chr, ke
h	(h is sometimes omitted) ch, wh, w, g (as in *Gila Monster*), ju (as in *San Juan*)
i	a, e, o, u, y, ei, uy, aye
ie	e, i, y, ee, ea, ei
ih	y, i, ei, ii
i	ch, g, dg, gg
ju (as in *San Juan*)	h, wh, ch
k	c, ch, g, gh, q, nk, cc, ck
kn (as in *knot*)	n, gn
kr	chr, cr, gr
ks	x
l	ll
lf (as in *calf*)	f, v, ph, pf, gh
ll	l, th
lm (as in *calm*)	m, mm, mb, mn
m	mm, lm, mb, mn, n
mb (as in *comb*)	mm, lm, mn
n	nn, ng, gn (as in *gnat*), kn, m
ng	n, nk, ch, k, q
nk	ng, ch, k, q
nn	n
o	a, e, l, u, aw, ow, eau (as in *beau*)
oey	oy, oe, o
oe	oy, oe, oey
oo	u, ow, ew
ou	u, au, ow, ew, oo
ow	au, ou, eau (as in *beau*)
oy	oi, oe, oey
p	b, pp, ph, bb
pf	f, pfph, gh, v, lf
ph	f, gh (as in *laugh*), pf, lf, p
ps (as in *psalm*)	s
q	c, ch, g, k, gh, cc, ck, ng, nk
r	rr, wr, rh
rh	r, rr, wr
rr	r, rh, wr
s	c, sh, tch, z, cz, ss, x
sch (as in *school*)	sh, s, sc, sk, sq
sch (as in *Schwarz*)	s, sh
sch (as in *Tisch*)	sh, tsh, tch, ch, cz, ti (as in *nation*), ss
sh	s, c, ch, cz, sch, ti (as in *nation*), ss
sk	sch, sh, s, sc, sq
sq	sc, sk, sch, sh
ss	s, c, ch, ci, sh, sc, z
t	d, dd, tt, th
tch	s, sh, c, ch, cz, s, tsh
th	t, tt, d
ti (as in *nation*)	sh, si, tsh, tch, ch
tj	i, g, ch, dh, dg, tch, tsch, s
tt	d, dd, t, th, dt ts, tz, cz, z, tzts, cz, z
u	a, e, i, omou, ew, oo
v	b, f, lf, w
w	wh, v, au, ow, h, ju (as in *San Juan*)
wh	w, h, ju (as in *San Juan*), oa
wr	r, rh, rr
x	s, z, ks, chs
y	i, e, ij
z	s, c, sh, sch, x, ds

Table 2.3: Frequently Misread Letters

A ....H, C, O		**n** ....u, a, o, ee, ie, ei, w, m	
a.........o, u, ei, ie, n, w		**O**.........C, U, V, D	
B.........R, P, S		**o** ....a, u, n, ee, ll, ie, ei, tt	
b.........li, le, t, h, t		**P**.........R, B, I, J, S, L	
C ....G, E, O, Ce		**p**.........ss, g, js, k, f, fs, fa, fi, fr	
c.........e, i, o, u		**Q**.........Z, D, I, J, G, C	
D.........G, S, I, J, T, Ir		**q**.........g, y, z, f, ej, ij, j	
d.........u, a, n, ie, ei, ee, ct, o		**R**.........Pi, B, S, Pe, Pr, Re	
E.........C, G, Ee		**r** ....e, s, i, ei, a	
e.........i, c		**S**.........L, I, i, St, Se, F, G, R, T	
ee.........u, fl, ll, a, o, ie, ei, w		**s** ....r, i, e, c	
F.........T, S, G, Ti, L		**sc** x	
f ....s, j, g, q, t		**ss**.........fs, p, rr, w, m, n	
G.........S, Q, Z, Cl, L, Se, Is		**T**.........F, S, L, D, Q	
g.........y, z, q, f		**t** ....l, f, Ir, i	
H.........N, W, He, Sl, St, A, F		**te**.........k	
h ....K, li, lc, le		**tt** ll	
I.........e, c, l		**U**.........V, A, O, N, H	
I.........S, T, F		**u** ....ee, a, o, n, ie, ei, ll, w	
I.........e, i, t		**V**.........N, W, Ir, ir, B	
ie.........ei, u, ee, n, a, o, w, il		**v** ....u, n, b, rr, s, r, o, ee, ei	
ll.........tt, ee, u, a, o, ie, ei		**W**.........M, N, U, H, St	
J.........I, L, S, Q, F, T, P		**w**.........m, rr, ur, nr, ui, ni, eu, en	
j.........y, g, f, q, z		**X**.........H, Z, N, J	
Jno.........Mr, Mo		**x**.........sc, c, r	
K ....H, R, B, tr, te		**Y**.........T, F, Z, Q	
k.........h, le, tr, te, R, B, H		**y**.........g, q, i, z, p, ej, ij, if	
M.........W, H, N, A, Al, Me		**Z**.........G, Q, Y	
m ....w, rr, ni, in, iv, ev, ai, ui, iu		**z**.........g, q, y, j, p	
N.........H, W, V, St, Ne			

3

Availability of the Census

After an army of clerks tallied every last detail and reports were sent off to various parties, the original Census Enumerators' Books were placed in storage. When the census records first started to become available to the public, they were only accessible in original form at the archives. This situation meant that only a limited number of people had access to the documents and that those originals were at risk of being damaged or lost through the constant handling.

As technology improved, archivists made an effort to further protect and preserve the original records. In the mid-twentieth century, the original census returns were microfilmed and distribution of these copies made the census more accessible than ever before. In recent years, advances in technology have it made it possible to create digital reproductions that can be viewed anywhere in the world using the Internet.

Today, census records, indexes, and images are available at many locations both online and off. Many people will prefer the instant success often offered in online indexes. Online indexes are typically the easiest to access and use. However, some people will find microfilm census records available offline more convenient and enjoyable. (Search strategies for both searching methods will be discussed in the next two chapters.) No matter which method of searching you prefer, the lists below include some of the most popular and accessible access points.

ONLINE ACCESS

Many groups have indexed and placed online various parts of the seven publicly available censuses (part- and whole-year indexes). Some groups offer these indexes for a fee, and some groups offer them for free. The sites mentioned below are a few of the most popular Internet sites used for accessing the census online.

ANCESTRY.COM

Ancestry.com is currently the only place online to find national indexes and images for the 1841 through 1901 censuses for England, Wales, the Channel Islands, and the Isle of Man. All of the indexes are linked to digital images of the original censuses scanned from microfilm. With all of the indexes in one place, you could potentially search all of the censuses in a single search. National indexes for the 1841 through 1901 censuses of Scotland are also available, but without corresponding images.

To use the index and images at Ancestry.com, visit <www.ancestry.com> or sister site <www.ancestry.co.uk>, which provides a localized pricing system for individuals residing in the United Kingdom. While you can search the indexes for free, you need a subscription in order to see the full index and the images.

BRITISHORIGINS

The Origins Network <www.originsnetwork.com> is comprised of several different sites. The BritishOrigins site <www.britishorigins.com> has partial indexes for 1841 and 1871 for England, Wales, the Channels Islands, and the Isle of Man. Images are available. You can purchase access for various lengths of time.

FAMILYHISTORYONLINE

While the Federation of Family History Societies (FFHS) has indexes for most census years, the places covered and the number of names included in each year is patchy. The FFHS site at <www.familyhistoryonline.net> is a central access point for the various census indexes created by societies and individuals. There are about 10 million records in total, with most of those coming from the 1851 and 1891 censuses. The collection is continually growing as indexes are added. Searching the indexes is free, but a small fee is charged to download a census entry. Images are not available.

FAMILYSEARCH

The 1881 census was the first UK census index available on the Internet. This index is the product of a collaboration of the Federation of Family History Societies and The Church of Jesus Christ of Latter-day Saints. Originally published on microfiche, in 1999 the data was taken from microfiche and put onto a collection of CDs. Later the index was made available on the Internet at <www.familysearch.org>. This index is entirely free at FamilySearch, but does not include any corresponding digital images.

FINDMYPAST.COM

Originally, the site 1837Online.com was dedicated to posting information about civil registration. Since their beginning they have also added indexes and images for the

1841, 1861, 1871, and 1891 censuses of England, Wales, Channel Islands, and Isle of Man. Recently they have changed their name to FindMyPast.com <www.findmypast.com/HomeServlet>. This is a pay-per-view service. Once you register, you can do a basic search for free, but you need to pay to see the full index or images.

FREECEN

Volunteers have contributed all of the indexes on <http://freecen.rootsweb.com>. The indexes are patchy, covering a variety of years and places all over England, Wales, the Channel Islands, Isle of Man, and Scotland. The site is constantly being updated, and you can visit the site for details of what is available. All searches and page views are free. Images are not available.

GENES REUNITED

A complete index with corresponding images for the 1901 censuses of England, Wales, the Channel Islands, and the Isle of Man is online at <www.genesreuinted>. The National Archives and a company called Qinetiq created this index. This site offers a free search of the index with a pay-per-view charge to view the full transcription and a separate charge to view the digital image.

SCOTLANDSPEOPLE

The General Register Office for Scotland has completed indexes for the 1841 to 1901 censuses of Scotland. The indexes are hosted on the GROS website <www.scotlandspeople.gov.uk>. All but the 1881 census include digital images. Credits must be purchased to view the index or images.

OFFLINE ACCESS

While the original census returns are safely stored at national archives in Scotland and England, full and partial microfilm copies of these documents are available through County Record Offices throughout the United Kingdom and through thousands of family history centers run by The Church of Jesus Christ of Latter-day Saints. Additional contact information for these and other research centers is available in appendix B, "Addresses to Libraries and Archives."

FAMILY HISTORY LIBRARY (FHL)

Located in Salt Lake City, Utah, the Family History Library is the largest library in the world dedicated to family history. The library was founded in 1894 by The Church of Jesus Christ of Latter-day Saints and is open to the public, free of charge. The library holds microfilm or microfiche copies of the 1841 to 1901 Scotland censuses and the 1841 to 1891 censuses for England, Wales, the Isle of Man, and the Channel Islands. The library's card catalog can be search at <www.familysearch.org>.

If a trip to Utah is not possible, film can be ordered through any of the branches of this library, called family history centers, located throughout the world.

To locate a family history center near you, visit <www.familysearch.org/Eng/Library/FHC/frameset_fhc.asp> and enter a location.

FAMILY RECORDS CENTRE (FRC)

The Family Records Centre is jointly run by the Office for National Statistics (ONS) and The National Archives (TNA). The centre provides access to a copy of all of the census years from 1841 to 1901 for England and Wales on either microfilm or microfiche. As of June 2006, The National Archives intends to move their staff and services from Myddelton Street, Islington, to the archives at Kew in 2008.

GENERAL REGISTER OFFICE FOR SCOTLAND (GROS)

Census records for Scotland from 1841 to 1901 are public and are held by the General Register Office for Scotland (GROS) at New Register House in Edinburgh. Very few of the returns from 1801 to 1831 have survived.

THE NATIONAL ARCHIVES (TNA)

The surviving census forms for England, Wales, the Channel Islands, and the Isle of Man are available at The National Archives (TNA) in Kew. The 1931 census schedules were destroyed in World War II. Very few of the returns from 1801 to 1831 have survived.

If you cannot travel to London, but you know the reference number for the England or Wales census page you would like to view, you can order a copy of the record from The National Archives. Visit The National Archives website to order copies of documents <www.nationalarchives.gov.uk/recordcopying/?source=ddmenu_shop3>. Researchers can obtain copies on paper or in a digital format.

COPYRIGHT

All copies of the census, whether original, microfilm, microfiche, or digital, are under Crown copyright. Limited numbers of copies can be made for personal or academic research, compilation of indexes, or educational purposes. Questions about copyright can be addressed to the Office of Public Sector Information <www.opsi.gov.uk>.

Permission is not required to use transcribed extracts from the returns.

Census on the Internet

There used to be no alternative to visiting a library or archive in order to view the census records. There has been tremendous progress in just the last few years in making the census easily available to the public. It started with family history societies putting existing surname and street indexes on CDs that could be viewed at home. These indexes on CDs were convenient, but researchers still had to view the records on microfilm if they wanted to see the handwritten returns.

Technology is changing the research process as well as accessibility of the census records. Recently, organizations have made national name-indexes and digital images of the records available on the Internet, on CDs, or sometimes on both. Now, not only can you access the complete national surname indexes from your own home, you can also see a digital image of the record. The complicated process of locating the right film has been reduced to a few steps on the computer. For some people this is the only way to search, while others still prefer the traditional microfilm approach (covered in chapter 5, "Accessing the Census on Microfilm").

ELECTRONIC INDEXES

One of the most exciting results of this new technology is that national indexes now exist for all publicly available census years. In addition, searches in an electronic index can provide more information in less time. Electronic indexes are also more powerful than paper indexes. As a researcher, you have the ability to search using important terms or criteria in many different combinations.

An index that exists in electronic form, rather than printed on paper, may be referred to as an electronic or digital index. The index may be stored as a spreadsheet, a text document, or a database. Anything that can be searched by a computer is an electronic index. Sophisticated database programs can store large amounts of data and allow users to easily search that information.

The usefulness of paper indexes is limited by the entries' arrangement. Order may be alphabetical or by some other grouping such as geography. If researchers want to view the data organized in different ways, multiple paper indexes with various orders have to be created.

An electronic index allows users to view the data in that index in myriad ways without re-creating or re-publishing the data. An electronic index also allows researchers to perform complex and powerful searches.

Consider using a paper index arranged alphabetically by surname to find a married woman whose husband's surname is unknown. Clearly, it would take a long time to review all of the given names and pick out all of the women with the sought-after given name. Even when all such women are identified, it is difficult to zero in on the specific woman you are seeking because paper indexes often do not include other identifying information, such as age.

On the other hand, most electronic indexes allow researchers to search for individuals with a specific first name, age, and birthplace. Such searching criteria can produce a short list of individuals who possibly match the person being sought.

A major benefit of an electronic index is the ability to search the entire country at once. If you don't know where an ancestor was residing during a particular census year, it is possible to search for someone with a particular name, within a particular age range, and get a list of possible matches. Or you can simply enter a surname and gather information showing where the majority of the people with that surname resided.

Electronic indexes can also show migration and social or demographic history. For instance, you can see how many people living in a certain county moved from some other county. If the occupation is included within an index, you can identify which occupation is most popular for any given surname. The potential uses for information in this accessible format are enormous.

Of course, electronic databases, like any other copy of the original, are bound to have errors. All of the same index errors described in chapter 2 can occur in electronic indexes. Keyed indexes are also susceptible to typing errors. For England and Wales, determine if a place is missing from the index, or is missing in the original using a reference such as the The National Archives Online Catalog <http://catalogue.pro. gov.uk>. See more details about the catalog in Chapter 5.

LOCATING CENSUS RETURNS

Fortunately, although there are many ways and places to view the census, the basic research method for using the census remains the same. Start your census search by identifying who you want to find, whether an individual or a family group. List all the known facts about that individual or family, such as name (including spelling variations of both given and surnames), nicknames, birth dates, names of parents, names of siblings, and likely residences. The more information you have when you begin the search, the easier it is to determine if you have found the correct person in the census later on. Review this information to identify the geographic area and time period in which to start searching.

The basic rule of thumb in census research is to start with the latest census when the individual would have been living. For example, if the death certificate for Joseph Spencer indicates that he died in 1858, look for him first in the 1851 census. From this point you can search back in time working from the known to the unknown, a standard for all genealogical research.

Sometimes we are so eager to push our research back in time and into the next generation that we are tempted to skip steps in the process. It may seem like you can save time by skipping years and finding the individual in the earliest census available. However, you may miss vital information by skipping over census years. One of the best ways to verify the accuracy of information found in a census is to compare it with other information gathered over time and see which answers are the most consistent. Collect information in every census year available and compare the results to get the best information possible.

Once the year to start with is established, identify the place to search by determining where your ancestor was most likely to have lived during the census. Census records include many different locations, but knowing the parish of residence will be the most useful. When it is used in reference to the census, the term parish usually refers to the civil parish in England and Wales and ecclesiastical parishes in Scotland. If you are looking for individuals residing in a very small town, you may need to consult a gazetteer to determine which parish would include it. For instance, Joseph Spencer lived in Swallow Hill, a place not listed in the census, but a gazetteer shows that Swallow Hill is a hamlet in Darton parish. This information re-focuses a census search on Darton.

Use other information sources such as family histories, civil registration certificates, trade directories, letters, or church records to find addresses and other residential information. Keep in mind that addresses on marriage certificates can be misleading. Sometimes the addresses were temporary, used only to establish residency. In large cities you may be misled by multiple streets that have the same name, a street that changed names, or a street that did not exist at the time of the census. Maps are very helpful for sorting this out. For some locations, additional finding aids give street names that have been altered or abolished. Check with local family history societies for more information.

That said, remember not to limit yourself by geographic boundaries. Do not disregard a location possibility just because it is in a different county than expected. People moved about in pursuit of jobs, when they married, and as the spirit moved them. Also, boundaries move over time and place names change. An individual may live in the same house, but may appear in different parishes on the census returns.

Once a year and place to start searching have been established, all that is left is to select the index to search. Several of the most popular digital indexes on the Internet are listed in Chapter 2. Whichever index is used, the basic principal will be the same.

As you search in the census, you are likely to find more than one potential match for the information you are researching, especially if the name is common, or you don't have very much information. Match as many pieces of information as you can to determine if you have located the correct individual. For example, if you find more than one person with the correct name and correct age, compare names of spouses, children, or siblings to verify that you have the right individual. Is the occupation correct? Is the birthplace correct? If you cannot verify the information, you may have to try and prove that one of the potential matches is not the right one by locating them in another census or other record that clearly shows whether they are the right individual.

Once the individual in question has been located, look at the neighbors on either side of the family. Neighbors can be useful in making connections within groups over time. Sometimes neighbors can turn out to be other family members or future family members. Taking a broader look at the neighborhood can give you an impression of the community life of your ancestors, such as average wealth, family size, and ethnic groups. In a small town, you should also consider extracting information for everyone with the surname you are looking for.

Once you have located your family in the census, print a copy of the census record or transcribe the information for your records. Remember to record where you located this information, including the URL if appropriate, so you or others can easily locate the page again if needed. Even if you do not find what you are looking for, make sure to keep a research log so that you do not repeat your efforts again later.

SEARCHING ELECTRONIC DATABASES

One of the challenges of using an electronic index is learning how to search it effectively.

Just because one search method works on one website does not mean it will work on all of them, although there are some basic steps that will apply to all. Read any helps or how-to guides about any index that is selected. These guides will usually contain hints and information about how to get the best results out of that particular index.

All digital indexes will have some kind of search template that must be filled in before a search can occur. A search template is usually a series of blank fields where information about the person being sought can be entered. Once the information is entered, the database will search for a match to that information. Success depends on both the accuracy of the index as well as understanding how to use it.

Most Internet sites will display a list of potential matches against the information provided. Selecting one of the possible matches will usually take you to either more information about that person or to a page that shows family members and\or neighbors. This information is just a transcription of the census, and it is best to view the census return if possible.

Here are some basic tips for getting the most results out of a census index on CD or on the Internet.

INCLUDE LESS INFORMATION

If you have too few search results or you did not find the person you were looking for on the first try, you may have included too much information. Many people will try to fill in every piece of information that they know. Some search engines, programs that search databases and report information that related to specific search criteria, will try to find a result that exactly matches everything you included in the search. As you search, try removing or changing some information. When removing information, it is best to start with information that is often incorrect or may not be exactly what you expect, such as a place name or surname.

TRY DIFFERENT COMBINATIONS OF INFORMATION

If you are not getting results, or at least not the results you expect, try looking for something different. Look for nicknames, alternate spellings, or other family members. You can even search some online indexes for a person of specific age and birthplace without including a name at all. You may need to be creative in your search approach to make sure you have really exhausted all possibilities.

TRY A WILDCARD SEARCH

A wildcard is a special character that is substituted for other letters and allows you to search for words that begin with the same stem. For example, some search engines use an asterisk to stand for zero to many characters. A search for *Wil** would return names such as *Will, William, Willis, Wills, Wild,* and *Wilde.* Wildcard searches can vary by search engine and website, so read available instructions or help files to understand what wildcard options are available.

ADD MORE INFORMATION

If you got too many results it is very likely that the name you are searching for is a common name or you have not included enough unique information. You can narrow your search results by adding additional information. Try adding items like birthplace, age, or known place of residence in different combinations and see if any yield better results.

WATCH FOR TRANSPOSED LETTERS

A common error is for typists to transpose letters. For example, try searching for *Goerge* instead of *George*. Occasionally letters are not only transposed, they are mistyped. Look at your keyboard to see what surrounding letters might have been typed instead. For example, if "d" was typed instead of "s," the surname Smith becomes Dmith.

DIGITAL CENSUS IMAGES

An index is never as good as the original image. Whenever possible, view the handwritten page yourself, whether a digital copy, a microfilm copy, or the original manuscript, after locating a person in an index to be sure that no information was missed or transcribed incorrectly. Some websites link their electronic images directly to the correct digital images. In such cases, once you find your ancestor in the electronic index, all you have to do is click a link to view the digital census image. You may run across electronic indexes that are not connected to digital images. In these instances, you will have to use the index information to find the correct images elsewhere.

Digital images can be created from either the original forms or from microfilm copies of forms. In some cases the digital images are cleaned up to make the text easier to read and to minimize the spots or streaks, called noise, that can sometimes be found on microfilmed census images.

Remember that electronic images are one more copy away from the original. Just as pages may have been skipped in microfilming, some pages may have been skipped when the microfilm or originals were scanned. If you think a page was skipped, you should look at the microfilm.

BENEFITS OF ELECTRONIC INDEXES AND DIGITAL IMAGES

There are many benefits to finding census images online. Perhaps the most obvious benefit of digital images is that you can search for your family's records anywhere that has an Internet connection at any time of the day. Many family historians appreciate the opportunity of discovering their family from the comfort of their own home.

Digital images are easily printed, saving time consuming transcription that often needs to be done when searching through microfilm. Printed digital images are often much clearer and easier to read than a photocopy of a microfilmed image.

You can easily save the images you find to your hard drive or insert them into your favorite family tree program. Some websites, such as Ancestry.com, allow you to save digital records to your account so that you can easily access them every time you visit the site.

Digital images are also more convenient to share with family, friends, and other family historians. It's much faster to e-mail a digital census image than it is to send a hard copy via ground mail. Some websites allow you to e-mail images you find just by clicking a link.

In addition, websites such as Ancestry.com also include areas where researchers can add comments to certain records—offering alternative information to what is found on the census sheet, such as corrected name spellings or more accurate ages.

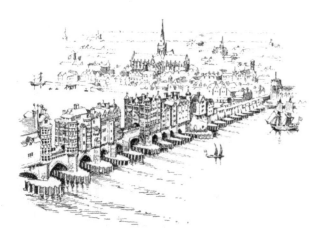

Accessing the Census
on Microfilm

Even with the many advantages of digital indexes, and digital copies of the images, there may be times where an alternate source may be a better option. Copies of the census in multiple formats are available at the Family Records Centre (FRC) in London, the General Register Office for Scotland (GROS) in Edinburgh, and the Family History Library (FHL) in Salt Lake City, as well as at many county record offices, family history centers, and other facilities throughout the world. Each facility may have a different cataloging system, which you need to learn to use, but ultimately all of the census records are organized according to their "home" archive. The home archive for returns from England and Wales is The National Archives (TNA), and for Scotland returns it is the GROS. In this chapter we will discuss the TNA reference system, the finding aids at the Family Records Centre, the GROS reference system, and the catalogue used at the Family History Library.

As discussed in chapter 4, start your census search by identifying who you want to find, whether an individual or a family group. Then you can locate any available finding aids to facilitate identifying the correct record on microfilm or microfiche.

Each archive, library, or county record office has its own set of finding aids, and you will have to determine what is available. Two of the most common and useful finding aids are street indexes and surname indexes. Many of the published finding aids for the British censuses were created in England or Scotland and therefore use the reference numbering system for the TNA, the GROS, or the local archive.

Find the reference number to locate the correct film using the catalog or finding aids available at the library you are using. Knowing the library or archive reference number often cuts steps out of the process at whichever library you visit. Obtaining as much of this information as possible before leaving home, by using Internet resources

STREET INDEX TO THE 1861 CENSUS ST GILES Street		TO FIND YOUR FILM Reference	TO FIND YOUR PLACE ON THE FILM Folios
Store Street, Gower Street	1-22	RG 9/171	29-33
	23-43	RG 9/171	56-60
	South Crescent	RG 9/171	76-77
, Little		RG 9/171	45
Streatham Street, Bloomsbury	1-3	RG 9/167	46-47
	Model Houses	RG 9/167	47-51
	Office	RG 9/167	47
Strickland Yard, Great Queen Street		RG 9/169	106
Tavistock Mews, Little Coram Street MISSING from ED4		RG 9/165	
Tavistock Street		RG 9/171	70-71
Tavistock Street, Tottenham Court Road	1-9	RG 9/172	2-4
	10-18	RG 9/171	69
Thompsons Yard, Southampton Row, Bloomsbury		RG 9/166	142
Thorney Street, Bloomsbury		RG 9/167	118-119
Tichbourne Court, High Holborn		RG 9/170	11-12
Torrington Lodge, Bloomsbury		RG 9/173	128-129
Torrington Mews, Bloomsbury		RG 9/173	127-128
, East, Bloomsbury		RG 9/166	52-53
Torrington Place, Bloomsbury	1-6	RG 9/173	126-127
see PANCRAS	7-8	RG 9/102	147-148
Torrington Square, Bloomsbury	1-34	RG 9/166	31-36
	37-40	RG 9/173	127
	41-71	RG 9/166	36-41
Torrington Street, Bloomsbury		RG 9/166	41
, Little, Bloomsbury		RG 9/166	41-42
Tottenham Court Road	196-208	RG 9/171	6-8
	209-226	RG 9/171	27-29
	227-258	RG 9/171	52-55
	259-268	RG 9/172	4
remainder see PANCRAS		RG 9/100 & 102	
Tower Street, Seven Dials		RG 9/173	99-112
Twyford Buildings, High Holborn	2-9	RG 9/170	34-36
Vernon Place, Bloomsbury	1-5	RG 9/167	68
	3	RG 9/167	95
	7-10	RG 9/166	124-125
Vine Street, Bloomsbury also called No 12 Broad Street	1 only	RG 9/167	123
Vinegar Yard, Shorts Gardens		RG 9/168	146
West Street, continuation of	North side 1-19	RG 9/173	91-95
Crown Street	South side see STRAND	RG 9/174	57-59

Figure 5.1. Street Index, 1861 Census [England and Wales].

or a library more local than the one you wish to visit, will save valuable time at the library for actual research.

STREET INDEXES

When searching in a large community, a street index can help you narrow down the area of town in which to focus the search. Street indexes list streets, terraces, lanes, and sometimes villages and hamlets in alphabetical order for a certain area, usually a registration district. Next to each street is listed the piece number and folio number, or range of folio numbers, of where the street appears in the census. Family history societies have published indexes for most cities with a population greater than 40,000.

In large cities, a street may cross multiple registration districts, and you need to check in all of them so that you do not miss part of the street. London, for example, is divided into about thirty-six registration districts. To locate streets in London, use a guide that shows which registration district a particular street is in, such as *Names of Streets and Places within the Metropolitan Area* published by the Metropolitan Board of Works in 1887 (see figure 5.1). Maps can also be helpful.

SURNAME INDEXES

One of the finding aids a researcher always hopes to find is a surname index. To use a surname index effectively you need to know the general location where your ancestors were living and of course their surname, including spelling variations. A surname index lists all of the surnames of the individuals within a certain area and the piece and folio numbers on which individuals with that surname appear. This reference number will allow you to go straight to the microfilm containing the census returns.

Some indexes also include the given (first) names of individuals. However, if given names are not listed and the surname is common, you may have to view several census returns before you find the correct entry. This is still easier than plowing through an entire city to locate someone. Family history societies have compiled most existing surname indexes and published them as booklets or, more recently, on CDs.

You will need to check what is available, although most societies indexed their county for the 1851 census. Recently, national indexes for all census years have been made available on the Internet.

In general, surname and street indexes can be located using Gibson's *Marriage, Census, and Other Indexes for Family Historians*. The indexes are available as booklets or in some cases as CDs. You can also check with the family history society that has interest in the county you are researching. The society may have copies of these indexes for use or for sale. The Federation of Family History Societies website is located at <www.ffhs.org.uk> and the Scottish Association of Family History Societies is found at <www.safhs.org.uk>.

PLACE NAME INDEX FOR 1871 CENSUS RETURNS

PLACE NAME	COUNTY ABBREV	DISTRICT NAME	DIST NO.	SUB D.No	STREET INDEX	NAME INDEX
Darrington	Yorks WR	Pontefract	503	3a		
Darsham	Suff	Blything	216	1b		
Dartford	Kent	Dartford	41	2a		
Dartington	Devon	Totnes	274	4a		
Dartmoor Forest	Devon	Tavistock	290	1c		
Dartmouth	Devon	Totnes	274	3		
Dartmouth St Petrox	Devon	Totnes	274	3		
Dartmouth St Saviour	Devon	Totnes	274	3		
Darton	Yorks WR	Barnsley	505	1		
Darwen	Lancs	Blackburn	474	6a	474	
Darwen, Lower	Lancs	Blackburn	474	6d	474	
Darwen, Over	Lancs	Blackburn	474	6a	474	
Datchet	Bucks	Eton	140	2a		
Datchworth	Herts	Hertford	133	1		
Dauntsey	Wilts	Malmesbury	243	1a		
Davenham	Ches	Northwich	449	4a		
Davenport	Ches	Congleton	450	1		
Daventry	Northants	Daventry	160	2a		
Davidstow	Corn	Camelford	290	2b		
Davington	Kent	Faversham	52	2b		
Davy Hall	Yorks ER	York	515	2b	515	
Daw End	Staffs	Walsall	372	4b		
Dawdon	Durh	Easington	547	1d		
Dawley	Salop	Madeley	350	1a		
Dawley Magna	Salop	Madeley	350	1a		
Dawlish	Devon	Newton Abbot	273	1c		
Daylesford	Worcs	Stow on the Wold	353	5		
Daywell	Salop	Oswestry	353	4b		
Deadwen Clough	Lancs	Haslingden	471	1d	471	
Deal	Kent	Eastry	62	4a		
Dean	Cumb	Cockermouth	571	3a		
Dean	Hants	Alresford	104	2		
Dean	Oxon	Chipping Norton	155	1b		
Dean Bottom	Kent	Dartford	41	2b		
Dean Mill, Little	Glos	Westbury on Severn	325	1g		
Dean Prior	Devon	Totnes	274	5		
Deane	Hants	Basingstoke	107	3		
Deanham	Northumb	Morpeth	559	1a		
Deanraw	Northumb	Hexham	556	3d		
Deansgate	Lancs	Manchester	467	2a	467	
Deanshanger	Northants	Potterspury	157	1b		
Dean, East	Glos	Westbury on Severn	325	1a		
Dean, East	Hants	Romsey	98	2		
Dean, East	Sussex	Westhampnett	82	6		
Dean, Little	Glos	Westbury on Severn	325	1a		
Dean, Netner	Beds	St Neots	169	2b		
Dean, The	Hants	Andover	109	4		
Dean, Upper	Beds	St Neots	169	2b		
Dean, West	Glos	Monmouth	578	1a		
Dean, West	Hants(pt)	Stockbridge	99	1		
Dean, West	Sussex	Westbourne	85	1		
Dean, West	Wilts	Alderbury	254	1b		
Dean, West	Wilts(pt)	Stockbridge	99	1		
Dearham	Cumb	Cockermouth	571	4e		
Debach	Suff	Woodbridge	214	4		
Debden	Essex	Saffron Walden	201	1		
Debdon	Northumb	Rothbury	564	1b		
Debenham	Suff	Bosmere	211	1a		
Deddington	Oxon	Woodstock	151	1a		
Dedham	Essex	Lexden	196	5		
Dedworth	Berks	Windsor	122	2d		
Deene	Northants	Oundle	165	2		
Deenethorpe	Northants	Oundle	165	2		
Deepcut	Surrey	Guildford	31	1b		
Deepdale	Yorks WR	Sedburgh	482	3		
Deeping	Lincs	Bourn	415	4		
Deeping	Lincs	Spalding	416	6		
Deeping Gate	Northants	Peterborough	166	3b		
Deeping St James	Lincs	Bourn	415	4		
Deeping St Nicholas	Lincs	Spalding	416	6		
Deeping, Market	Lincs	Bourn	415	4		
Deeping, West	Lincs	Stamford	414	2		
Deerhurst	Glos	Tewkesbury	336	1		
Defford	Worcs	Pershore	383	1		
Deighton	Yorks ER	York	515	5	515	
Deighton	Yorks WR	Northallerton	534	1		
Deighton, Kirk	Yorks WR	Wetherby	489	1a		
Deighton, North	Yorks WR	Wetherby	489	1b		
Delamere	Ches	Northwich	449	1a		
Delamere	Corn	Camelford	290	2c		
Delly End	Oxon	Witney	152	3a		

Page number 68

Figure 5.2. Index to Place Names, 1871, England, Wales, Channel Islands, Isle of Man.

Once you have decided which year and place you are going to view, determine whether a surname or street index exists. Prior to censuses' availability on the Internet, when finding aids did not exist, researchers had to view the census by place and page-by-page. You may still have to view a census page-by-page when an index is inaccurate, but it is not as common a task.

FINDING AIDS AT THE FAMILY RECORDS CENTRE

To find census records in England or Wales at the Family Records Centre (FRC), first determine whether there is a street or surname index for the place and census year you wish to search. If you are at the Family Records Centre, you can consult the reference book *Index to Surname Indexes (By Place)*. This book contains an alphabetical list of places for which the FRC has a surname index.

If a street or surname index is not available, or you do not know in which registration district to find a place of interest, start your search with the place-name index (see figure 5.2). This is an alphabetical list of most places in each census year. The place-name index does not include every populated place in the country. You may need to consult a gazetteer or map if you do not find the specific place you are looking for. Once you locate the place of interest, the place-name index shows the corresponding county, registration district, registration district number, sub-district number, and indicates whether a street or surname index exists at the FRC.

After looking at the place-name index, take the registration district name and number from the place-name index and turn to the series list that corresponds to that year. The series list is a list of places ordered by registration district number. Locate the district by number, and you will see what piece number includes that district, as well as a list of sub-districts, civil parishes, and towns. The order in which places appear in the series list shows what order these places will most likely appear on the film. (The place-name index for 1841 gives the page number to look up in the series list.)

The 1871 census place-name index shows that the parish of Darton is in district 505 (figure 5.2). The 1871 census series list shows that Registration District 505 is the district of Barnsley; includes Cudworth, Carlton, Darton, Notton, Roystone, and Woolley; and is part of piece 4643 in the 1871 census (see figure 5.3).

The series list also indicates if a parish is in more than one district or piece. Comments will indicate if a piece is missing or damaged in the original. Finally, certain numeric codes in the list can let you know if there are any unusual returns in that piece (in figure 5.3, the "(4)" appearing in the line for piece 4644 indicates that the returns for a hospital are included in that piece). These codes are as follows:

1. Barrack and military quarters
2. HM ships at home

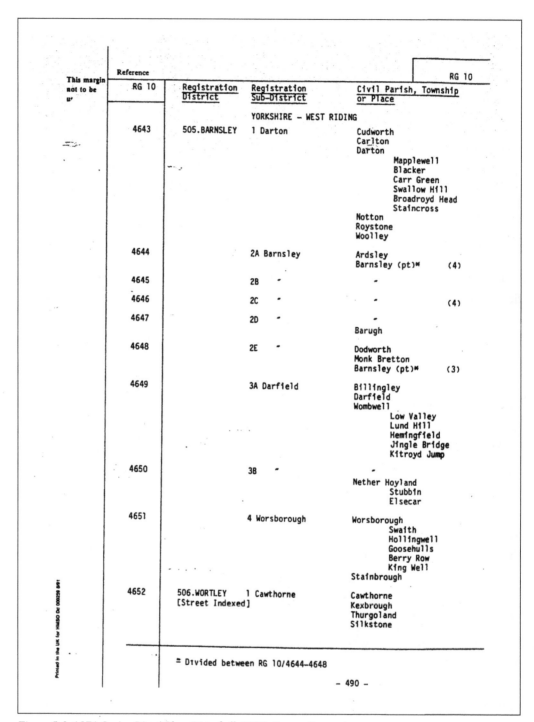

Figure 5.3. 1871 Series List (*Class List of all 1871 Census Returns*).

42

3. Workhouses (including pauper schools)

4. Hospitals (sick, convalescent, incurable)

5. Lunatic asylums (pubic and private)

6. Prisons

7. Certified reformatories and industrial schools

8. Merchant vessels

9. Schools

The series lists are available as books at the FRC, but you can also get the same information when you use The National Archives Online Catalogue <http://catalogue.pro.gov.uk>. You will save time at the library if you can use this catalogue to complete some of these preliminary steps from home.

To search The National Archives Online Catalogue for a place name:

1. Click "Search the Catalogue" at the top left of the screen to bring up a search template.

2. Enter the place name of interest in the field labeled "Word or phrase." Narrow down the search by entering in the "Department or Series Code" field the class number for the census you want to search (HO for 1841 and 1851; RG for 1861–1901).

3. Click "Search."

The results of the keywords you searched for will be returned. All the reference information that you need is on this screen. For more details, view the catalog entry for that parish by clicking the item that most closely matches the information you are seeking.

As with the printed series list, comments indicate if the piece is damaged or missing (a list of missing and damage pieces is included in appendix F). In some cases, you will find a single parish listed in multiple counties. If you do not find what you are looking for in the original parish you were searching, you can try searching in nearby parishes listed in the series list.

Remember not to limit yourself by geographic boundaries. Do not disregard a location possibility just because it is in a different county than expected. Remember that census registration districts frequently overlapped county boundaries.

THE NATIONAL ARCHIVES REFERENCE SYSTEM

Each page of the census for England and Wales can be located easily using a unique reference number. TNA reference numbers are made of three main components. For example, a typical reference number may appear as RG12\436, f.82. The first part of the reference number, RG12, is the class number. When the census records were deposited at The National Archives, the records for each year were assigned a class code indicating the record group and the series number. The returns for the 1841 and 1851 censuses both fall in record group HO (Home Office). All of the other census years are filed in record group RG (Registrar General). The reference numbers for each census year are:

- 1841—HO 107 (pieces 1–1465)
- 1851—HO 107 (pieces 1466–2531)
- 1861—RG9
- 1871—RG10
- 1881—RG11
- 1891—RG12
- 1901—RG13

The second part of the reference number, in this example 436, is the piece number. Piece numbers were assigned by geography, starting in the south and winding northward through the country. The counties of England are first, followed by the counties of Wales. In 1841 the census returns for England and Wales are arranged alphabetically by county and then by parish.

The third and final part of the reference number is a folio number. Together, these three pieces of information provide unique information that identifies a specific set of pages in the census. Finding aids and catalogs will help you determine the reference number that you need to guide you to the census page you want to view. In 1841, the reference number will also include a book number.

USING CENSUS RECORDS AT THE GENERAL REGISTER OFFICE FOR SCOTLAND

When using the Scottish census you will use the same basic approached outlined above. Start by identifying the name and number for the parish of interest. Find out what census indexes exist using Peter Ruthven-Murray's *Scottish Census Indexes: Covering the 1841–1871 Civil Censuses.*

Even if an index does not exist, you can still locate the film that you need. The Scottish census is arranged alphabetically by county and then by parish for 1841–1871. In 1881 and 1891, the parishes are arranged strictly by parish number.

THE GENERAL REGISTER OFFICE FOR SCOTLAND REFERENCE SYSTEM

The GROS citation format includes registration or parish number, enumeration district number, entry number, and census year. For example, a reference might be given as 183/1/24/1861 (see figure 5.4). This indicates that the person or family is found in the 1861 returns, in parish 183, enumeration district 1, and line 24. In 1851, the reference number does not include the parish number, so for this year only you need to also include the parish name. If the citation refers to a library or archive other then GROS, include the film number from that library.

USING CENSUS RECORDS AT THE FAMILY HISTORY LIBRARY

Copies of the series list for England and Wales described above are also available at the Family History Library (FHL) in Salt Lake City. While obtaining the TNA or GROS reference number is helpful, you will still need to find the film number that is used at the FHL. To find a film number at the Family History Library, or at a local family history center, use the Family History Library Catalog. This is available on microfiche, on CD, or online at FamilySearch <www.familysearch.org>.

To use the catalog online go to <www.familysearch.org>. Click the "Library" tab. On the new page, click "Family History Library Catalog" at the top of the screen.

To search for a place name:

1. Click the "Place" button to bring up a search template.
2. Enter the place name you are looking for.
3. If more than one place with that name is returned, choose the correct place.
4. Click the Search button to get a list of topics.
5. Choose the topic of "Census" and the year, if it is listed. If a surname or street index exists, it is listed under the topic "Census-Index."

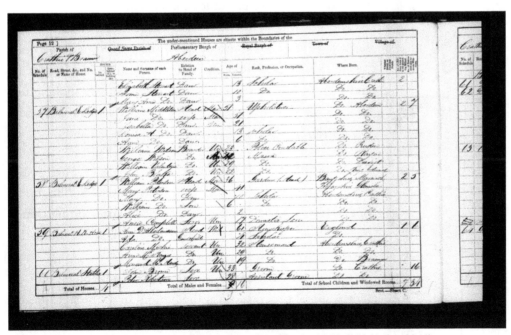

Figure 5.4. John Brown, a groom in the Balmoral Stables in 1861 (183/1/24/1861).

Figure 5.5.
Filming strip.

6. Click the "View film notes" button to see a list of film numbers for the various census years for that place.

7. Choose the film to view and make notation of the reference number.

One roll of microfilm can include several places. The description of each film includes the piece number, or parish number in Scotland, so that you can more easily find your spot on the film. In England and Wales, if a piece number is not indicated it means that you will need to inspect the entire film. Write down the film number and any other numbers, for future reference. The film number is also the information you need to order film into your local family history center.

Another quick reference tool at the Family History Library is a book commonly referred to as *The Census Register.* The full title of this resource for England and Wales is the *Index of Place Names Showing the Library Microfilm Numbers for the 1841–1891 Census of England, Wales, Isle of Man, and Channel Islands.* Find the place name in the alphabetical list. The columns to the right of the place name list the Family History Library call numbers for the 1841 through 1891 census microfilms that include the piece or parish for that location.

The full title of the Census Register for Scotland is the *Index to Parishes or Districts in the Census of Scotland for the years 1841–1891.* The register is organized alphabetically by county and then by parish. Find the place name you are looking for, and the parish number and Family History Library call number for the film will be listed next to the place name.

FROM REFERENCE TO FILM

Once you have determined the correct microfilm using one of the methods previously described, load the film on a microfilm reader. To find your place on the film, first locate the correct piece or parish number.

There may be multiple pieces, in sequential order, on one film. A slip of paper placed at the bottom or to the side of each census return has either the TNA or GROS reference number printed on it; this will help you locate the piece, parish, or other place of interest on the film. For example, figure 5.5 shows that the census page is in HO 107 piece 2128.

For England and Wales, if you used a finding aid such as a street index or a surname index, you should also have a folio number to look up. Folio numbering starts over with each new piece and then runs sequentially through each piece. A folio is defined as a two-sided piece of paper, where each side counts as one page. In the census, the folio number appears on every other page as a rubber-stamped number. This number is usually in the upper right hand corner of the piece of paper and appears on the first of the two sides/pages. Folio numbers were added before filming the manuscripts. Because a folio refers to two sides of a piece of paper, the person you are looking for could be on either side.

The reference system for the 1841 census is a little different than the one used in other census years. In 1841, each piece is divided into books and the folio numbers are numbered sequentially within each book. As a result, folio numbers repeat within each piece and cannot be used as a unique reference number. The book number is handwritten, and it appears on the first instructional page of each book. The number appears as a fraction where the piece number is written above a line and the book number underneath. In figure 5.6, the book is book number one of piece 856. In some of the microfilmed copies, the book appears as part of the reference number on the filming strip.

If you do not have a folio number, you will need to read each page of each piece in the census to find who you are looking for. You can narrow your search by locating the most likely place of residence. Remember that towns will appear in roughly the order they appeared in the series list. Each piece is divided into enumeration districts. At the beginning of each Census Enumerator's Book, there are several pages of instructional and descriptive material (see figures 5.6–5.12). Read the page that describes the area covered in the enumeration district, usually the first or second page, to determine if the enumeration district is of interest to you. Parishes can span multiple enumeration districts. You may need to look at each page within several enumeration districts to locate the person you are looking for. If you do not find the person you are seeking in the expected parish, expand your search to nearby towns and parishes.

Vessel, institution, and military returns use the same system of reference numbers. One difference is that descriptions of vessels often follow the personal information for passengers. The series list or TNA catalog can help you locate those institutions within the place of interest.

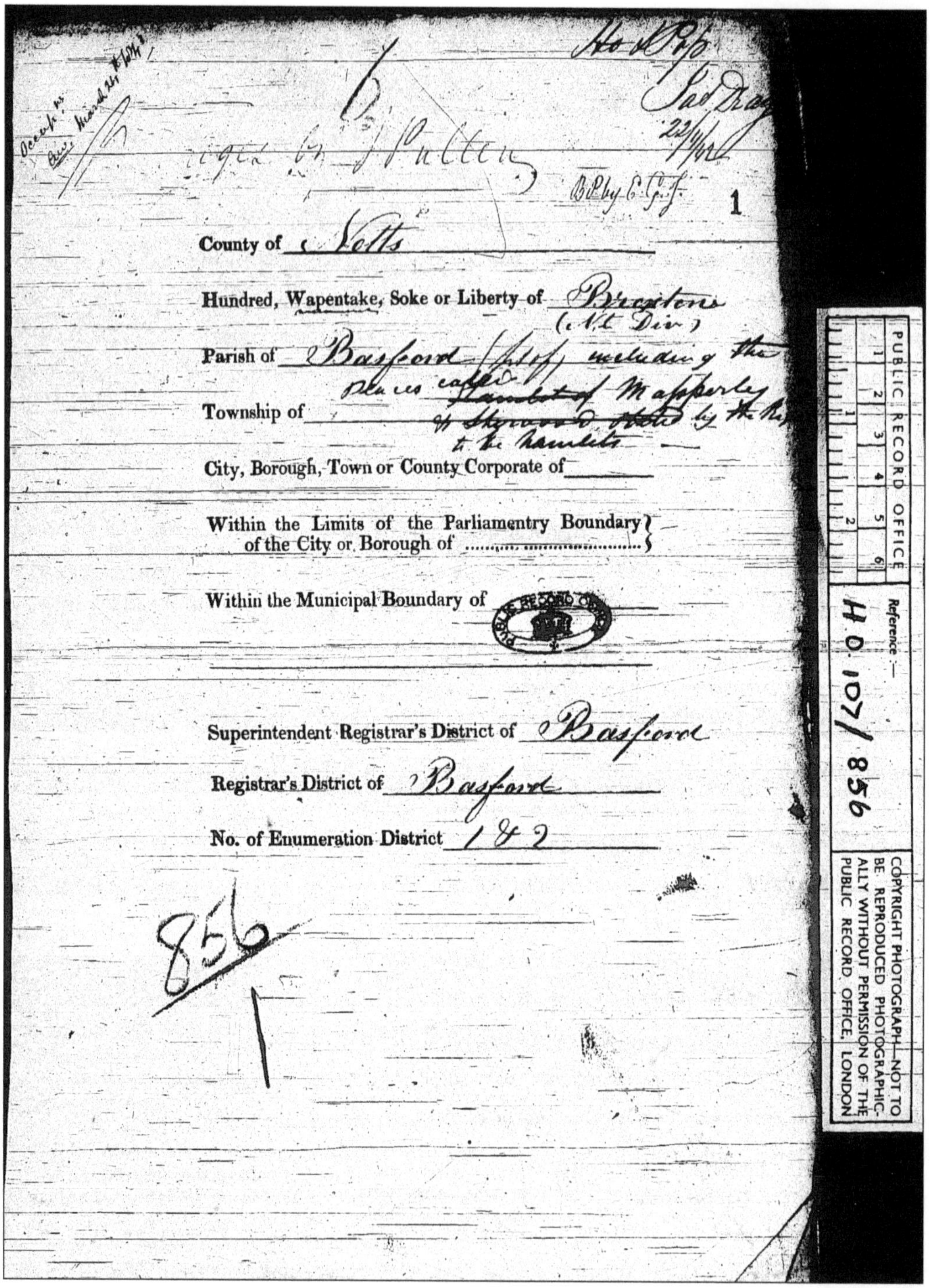

1

County of Notts

Hundred, Wapentake, Soke or Liberty of Broxtowe

Parish of Basford

Township of

City, Borough, Town or County Corporate of

Within the Limits of the Parliamentry Boundary of the City or Borough of ....

Within the Municipal Boundary of

Superintendent Registrar's District of Basford

Registrar's District of Basford

No. of Enumeration District 1 & 2

856

Figure 5.6. Title page in 1841 showing book number (HO 107\856, b.1, f.1).

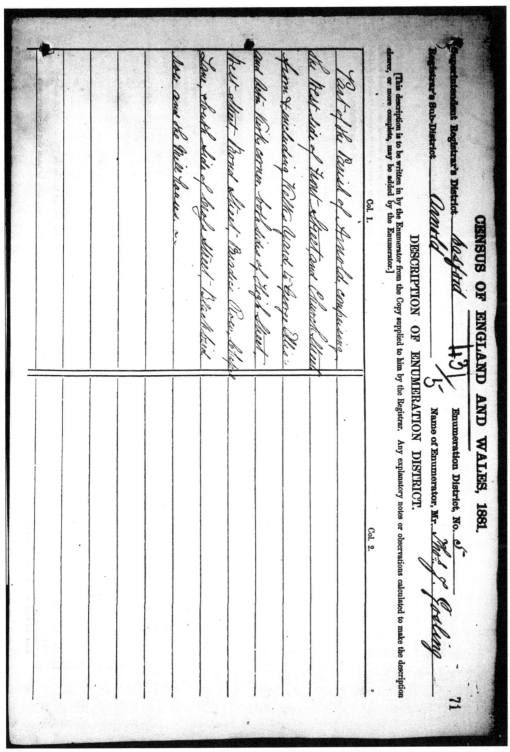

Figure 5.7. Title page and description of Census Enumerator's Book (RG11\3336, f.71, p.i).

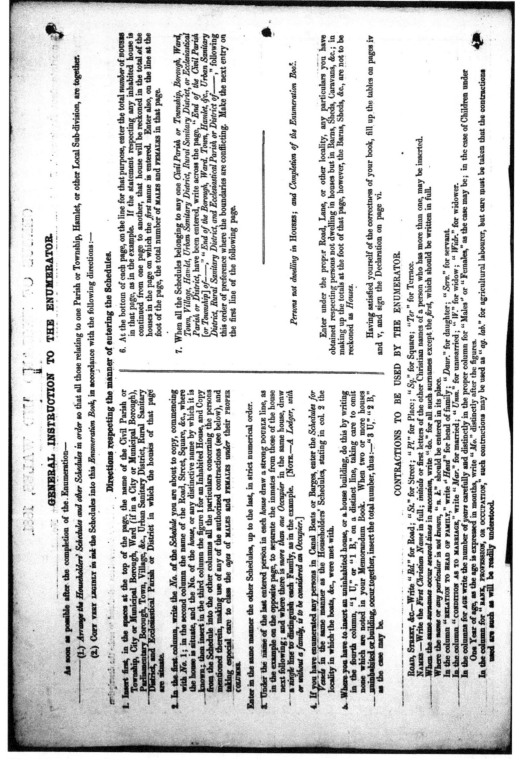

Figure 5.8. Instruction to the enumerator from Census Enumerator's Book (RG11\3336, f.71, p.ii).

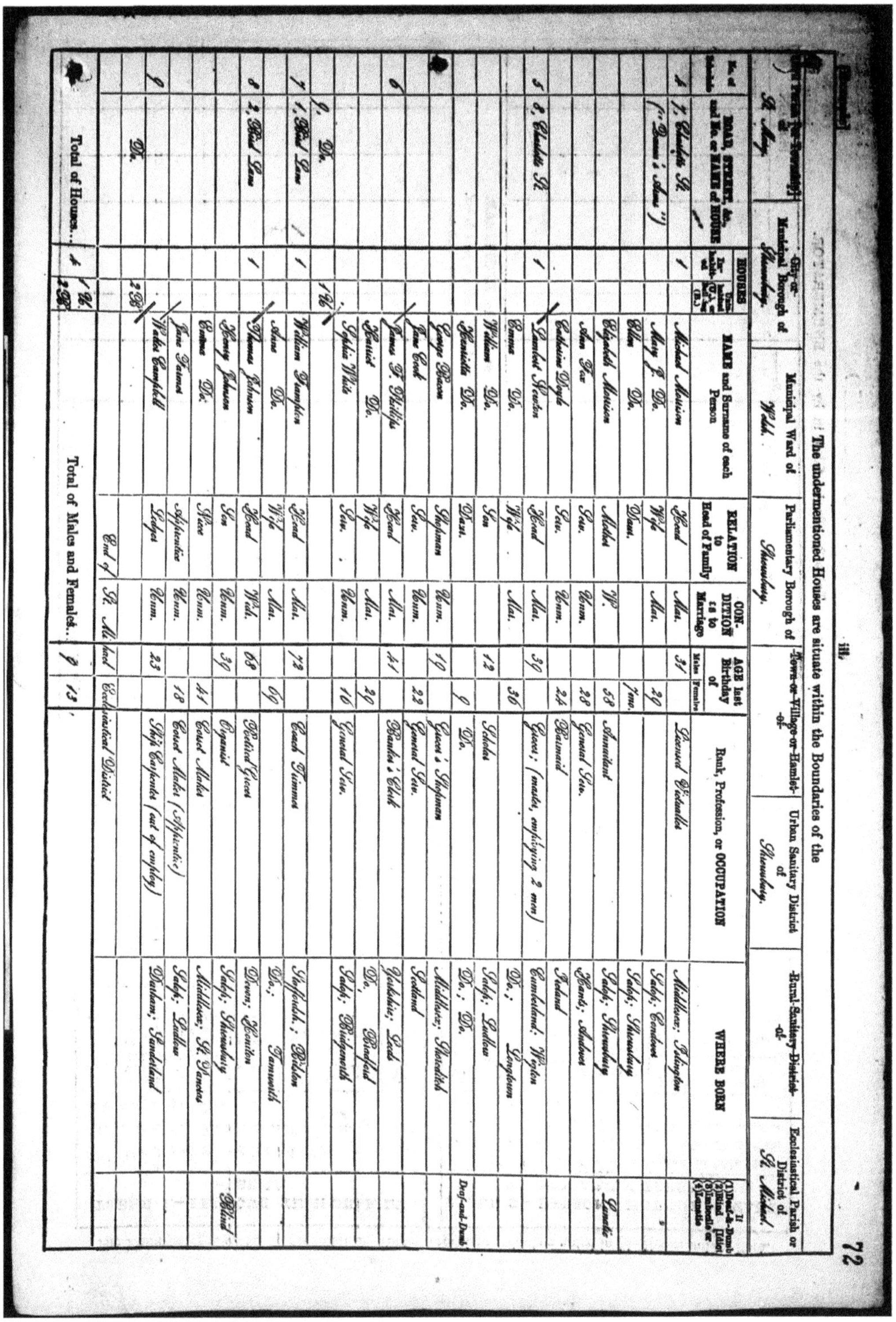

iii. 72

The undermentioned Houses are situate within the Boundaries of the

Civil Parish [or Township] of	City or Municipal Borough of	Municipal Ward of	Parliamentary Borough of	Town or Village or Hamlet of	Urban Sanitary District of	Rural Sanitary District of	Ecclesiastical Parish or District of
St. Mary	Shrewsbury	Welsh	Shrewsbury		Shrewsbury		St. Michael

No. of Schedule	ROAD, STREET, &c., and No. or NAME of HOUSE	HOUSES Inhabited	HOUSES Uninhabited (U.), or Building (B.)	NAME and Surname of each Person	RELATION to Head of Family	CONDITION as to Marriage	AGE last Birthday of Males	AGE last Birthday of Females	Rank, Profession, or OCCUPATION	WHERE BORN	If (1) Deaf-and-Dumb (2) Blind (3) Imbecile or Idiot (4) Lunatic
4	7, Charlotte St.	1		Michael Morrison	Head	Mar.	31		Licensed Victualler	Middlesex; Islington	
	("Dawn's Arms")			Mary J. Do.	Wife	Mar.		29		Salop; Condover	
				Ellen Do.	Daur.			7mo.		Salop; Shrewsbury	
				Elizabeth Morrison	Mother	W.		58	Annuitant	Salop; Shrewsbury	Lunatic
				Ann Fox	Serv.	Unm.		28	General Serv.	Hants; Andover	
				Catherine Doyle	Serv.	Unm.		24	Barmaid	Ireland	
5	8, Charlotte St.	1		Lambert Newton	Head	Mar.	39		Grocer; (master, employing 2 men)	Cumberland: Wigton	
				Emma Do.	Wife	Mar.		36		Do.; Longtown	
				William Do.	Son		12		Scholar	Salop; Ludlow	
				Henrietta Do.	Daur.			9	Do.	Do.; Do.	Deaf-and-Dumb
				George Bacon	Shopman	Unm.	19		Grocer's Shopman	Middlesex; Shoreditch	
				Jane Cook	Serv.	Unm.		22	General Serv.	Scotland	
6				James F. Phillips	Head	Mar.	41		Banker's Clerk	Yorkshire; Leeds	
				Harriet Do.	Wife	Mar.		29		Do. Bradford	
				Sophia White	Serv.	Unm.		16	General Serv.	Salop; Bridgenorth	
	9. Do.		1U								
7	1, Bird Lane	1		William Frampton	Head	Mar.	72		Coach Trimmer	Staffordsh.; Bilston	
				Anne Do.	Wife	Mar.		69		Do.; Tamworth	
8	2, Bird Lane	1		Thomas Johnson	Head	Widr.	68		Retired Grocer	Devon; Honiton	
				Henry Johnson	Son	Unm.	39		Organist	Salop; Shrewsbury	Blind
				Emma Do.	Niece	Unm.		41	Corset Maker	Middlesex; St. Pancras	
				Jane Farmer	Apprentice	Unm.		18	Corset Maker (Apprentice)	Salop; Ludlow	
9				Walter Campbell	Lodger	Unm.	23		Ship Carpenter (out of employ)	Durham; Sunderland	
	Do.		2B								
					End of	St. Mi	chael	Eccle	siastical District		
	Total of Houses...	4	1U. 2B.	Total of Males and Females...			9	13			

Figure 5.9. Example page from Census Enumerator's Book (RG11\3336, f.72, p.iii).

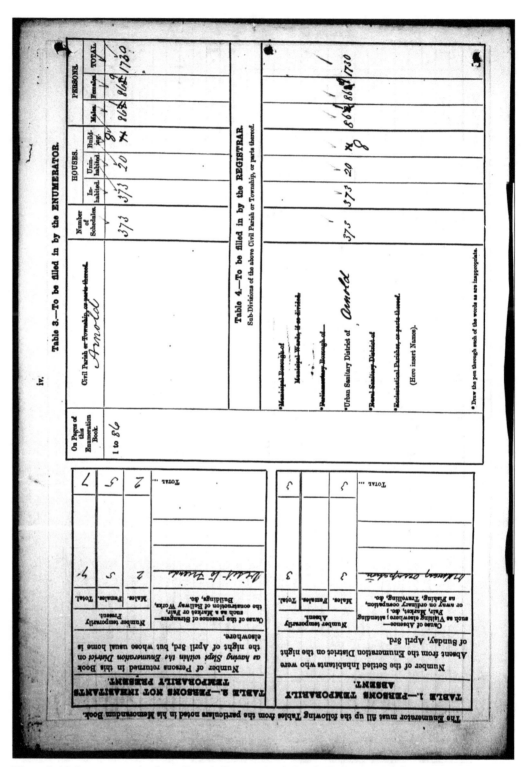

Figure 5.10. Summary page from Census Enumerator's Book (RG11\3336, f.72, p.iv).

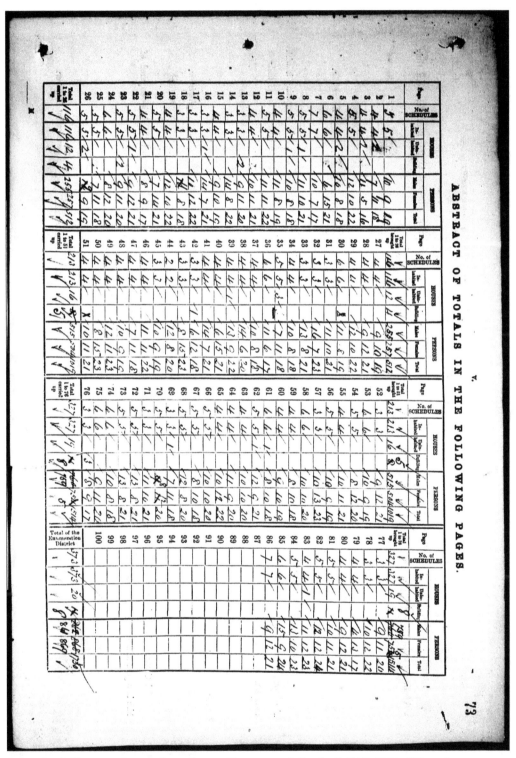

Figure 5.11. Abstract of totals from Census Enumerator's Book (RG11\3336, f.73, p.v).

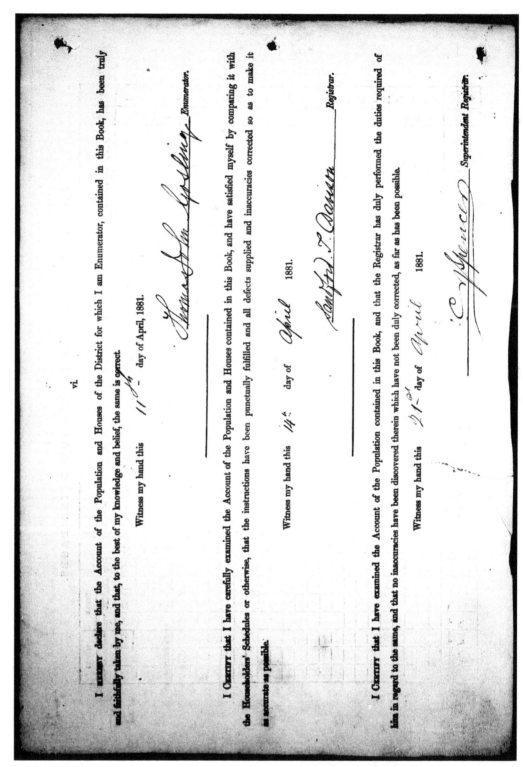

Figure 5.12. Declaration of accuracy from Census Enumerator's Book (RG11\3336, f.73, p.vi).

6

Using and Interpreting Census Records

Congratulations, you have finally found the people you were looking for! So now what? Now you need to interpret the information and combine it with what you already know. Understanding what questions were asked and how the answers were recorded will help you apply the information correctly.

NUMBERS AND TALLY MARKS

The first columns on most census forms are for the schedule number, street name, and address. The schedule number indicates the order in which the enumerator copied the records and does not usually correspond to a physical address. The street name and address may reflect the actual address but is not always exact (see chapter 2). This information can help you place neighbors together.

The clerks who tallied the numbers for the census's original purpose made heavy marks through valuable information. While most of the marks made by the census officials appear to be random and written through important information, some marks can be very helpful. On the line forming the left border of the Name column, you will often see a series of hash marks. The marks actually serve a useful purpose. Each new house or building is indicated by a slash (\) and each double slash (\\) indicates the start of a new family. Because relationships were not recorded in 1841, the hash marks are very useful for establishing family groups. In 1851, clerks underlined the last member of the family, rather than using the hash marks.

NAMES

The name column is one of the most exciting columns on the form since the name is what gives identity and personality to the individual. Names are also the main point of linking people together. Given names may be repeated in different generations of the family, and an ancestral surname might be used as a middle name. If you see a middle name that shows up as the neighbor's surname, you may want to investigate a possible connection. You can also use other records to make connections with names. Check the names of witnesses on marriage certificates or wills. Even if they are not related, it is interesting to see which neighbors played a role in your ancestors' lives.

Names are also maddeningly inconsistent. In 1841, the enumerators were not required to give full Christian names. Enumerators often recorded only the first name and middle initial or only initials. It is also very common to find only initials listed in institutions. Name variations must always be considered when searching in the census.

Another thing to remember about names is that the name recorded on the census can depend on who answered the questions. For example, a parent may enter nicknames for children or a person might use a middle name instead of given name. On the other hand, a person may use a nickname for most of his life, but record his full given name on the census. For instance, Aunt Dotty may have given her name as Dorothy on the census.

Nicknames, or alternate names, are not always obvious, so do some investigations to see what possible variations there might be. Nicknames can be derived from rhyming words, physical traits, shortening a name or exchanging letters in the name. Polly, for example, can be a nickname for Mary. In Scotland, you may even find names in Gaelic, which look nothing like the English version of the name. Some good reference books are Dunkling's *Scottish Christian Names: An A–Z of First Names* as well as *The Oxford Dictionary of English Christian Names* by Elizabeth G. Withycombe.

Spelling rules were not as rigid as they are today. Your ancestor may have not been literate and could have written his name phonetically, or the enumerator could have made an error in the copy. Given names and even family names may be spelled differently from one census to the next.

Surnames can be just as variable as given names. There may be more than one family with the same surname within the same location. Occasionally, women, especially widows, might be listed under their maiden names. It is even possible that the surname is completely incorrect, either because of a clerical error, or it was just reported differently. The change may be as subtle as Whitehead one year and Whitehall the next, or as dramatic as Freeman on one report and Raymond on another. Whether there are many families with your surname, or one that doesn't have the right surname, but is otherwise correct, check all possibilities, comparing addresses, ages, and birthplaces and so on, against other sources to determine if the family is "your" family.

RELATIONSHIPS

The 1851 to 1901 censuses include relationships of individuals to the head of the house, which is extremely helpful when constructing family units. Some of the terms used in the relationship field may be misleading if they are not applied in context with other known facts. For example, the relationship *son-in-law* may be used in modern terms, but it could also indicate that the child is a stepson. Other, more subtle, differences are found in relationships. For instance, a *boarder* is someone who dines with the family while a *lodger* does not. Occasionally the answers may even describe a relationship as *friendly*.

Common abbreviations for relationships:

Daur. for Daughter

S. for Son

Serv. for Servant

Because the recorded relationships are to the head of the house only, use caution when inferring relationships between other people in the house. Take clues from the ages and birthplaces of family members to determine the possible relationships. For example, a woman who is recorded as the wife of the head of the house may not be the mother of all the children in the home. If there is a large gap between the ages of the children, or if the children are too old to have been born from that woman, this may indicate that she is a second wife and some or all of the children are her stepchildren. The relationship column only indicates the head of the house has sons and daughters, but not how they are related to the wife.

Occasionally you find that the enumerator was confused as to which person was the head of the house, especially when families live together, and marked a woman as *wife* when she was really the wife of the son and should be listed as *daughter-in-law*. You might also find an individual listed as a child one year but as a grandchild in the next. Such inconsistencies are one of many reasons why there is such value in looking at every census.

Relationships in some returns from Wales are written in Welsh (see figure 6.1). Some common relationships include the following:

- Pen Teula (Head)
- Wraig (Wife)
- Mab (Son)
- Merch (Daughter)
- Bryddiwr (Brother)
- Chwaer (Sister)
- Gwas (Servant)

MARITAL STATUS

The answer regarding marital status is usually abbreviated as follows:

- Mar. for Married

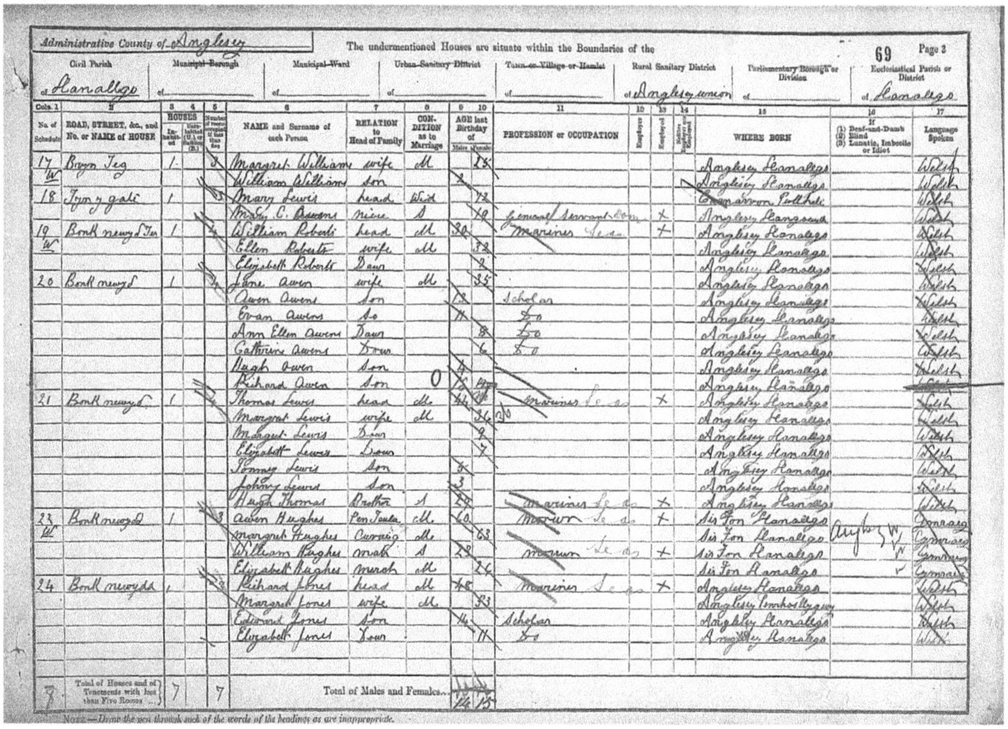

Figure 6.1. 1891 census page from Wales (RG12\4675, f.69, p.3).

- S. for Single
- W. or Widr. for Widowed or Widower

These status indicators can help you identify life events that happened between census years. An example of this would be a woman listed as single in one census and as a widow in the next census. One conclusion might be that she was married and widowed between census years, leading to further research for marriage and death records.

AGES

When trying to match someone's age, you should always allow a difference of several years on either side of the reported age. In some cases the persons completing the form may not have known their age or the age of others in the household. Others may have hidden their true age.

Ages in 1841 are especially prone to error. Enumerators were instructed to round down ages for individuals over fifteen to the nearest five. Therefore, a person from age twenty to twenty-four would be recorded as age twenty, while a person from age twenty-five to twenty-nine would be recorded as twenty-five.

Ages can be used to gauge family completeness and establish a time line. In an average nineteenth century family, children were generally born about every two years. If

Table 6.1.
Some Common Abbreviations for Occupation:

Ag. Lab.	Agricultural Laborer
Ap.	Apprentice
Cl.	Clerk
Dom.	Domestic
F.S.	Female Servant
F.W.K.	Framework Knitter
Ind.	Independent Means
J.	Journeyman
Lab.	Laborer
M.S.	Male Servant
M.	Manufacturer
m.	maker, as in *Dress m.*
N.K.	Not Known
Rail. Lab.	Railway Laborer
Serv.	Servant

there is a gap in the ages of the children larger than two or three years, it may indicate a child in the family who is not listed on the census form. You might also find children who are too old to be children of the woman listed as the wife in the family. Taken together, the pieces of information might suggest that the woman listed as the wife in the family is not the mother of the children. Very young children living with an older couple may actually be illegitimate children being raised by their grandparents.

OCCUPATIONS

Deciphering occupations and the abbreviations used for them can be challenging. It seems that occupations are as unique as the people who fill them. Occupations recorded in the census range from "Dowager Empress" to "magician" to simply "boy."

Starting in 1861 children over five years old were given the occupation "scholar" if they were attending school daily.

Occupations can lead to other records with additional information, such as apprenticeship and military records. Unfortunately, occupations are also heavily abbreviated or may be unfamiliar terms even when written out. Table 6.1 includes some common abbreviations for occupations. A list of abbreviations is also given in the enumerator's instructions and an even more detailed list of possible terms is available in *Guide to Census Reports, Great Britain, 1808–1966.*

Despite all of their instruction, enumerators must have been at a loss to identify those people who entered *magician* or the like as their occupation. Descriptions of jobs with unusual or outdated names can be found in occupation dictionaries. Some occupations do not seem unusual at first but actually have a hidden meaning. For instance, *dressmaker* was a common euphemism for prostitute. This does not mean that every female who gave her occupation as dressmaker is a prostitute, but other clues may lead you to that conclusion.

BIRTHPLACES

Birth locations are quite important in family history research since they are helpful for building a time line as well as acting as a first step into other record types. Birthplaces can place the person on the census in a specific location decades before the census was ever taken. The birthplaces of children in a family can show whether that family migrated over time. For example, you might find a family where the parents and the oldest child were born in one location and the rest of the children were born in the current location. This tells you that the family moved at least once, at that you can check in the first parish for the marriage of the parents, as well as other children who may have been born in that parish.

In the 1841 census the only birthplace information is whether the person was born in the county of residence, outside the county of residence, in another country in Britain, or in a foreign country. Countries within Great Britain are recorded using the abbreviations "S" for Scotland, "I" for Ireland, "E" for england and "W" for Wales.

However, enumerators are not known for their consistency when following instructions, so it is always worth checking additional census returns to see if they happened to record more detailed information in other years. Sometimes, not following the rules can work in your favor. For instance, an enumerator may actually record the name of a town in a foreign country even if it wasn't required.

From 1851 onward, the birthplace is usually listed with the county name first and then the parish within that county. If you are new to English geography some unexpected county abbreviations you may find are Oxon. for Oxfordshire, Salop. for Shropshire, and Hamps. for Southampton.

Unfortunately, birthplaces are often inaccurate. Town names can have a variety of spellings or can be shortened, which leads to confusion about the actual place. This is especially common in Wales where place names are long and can look the same once they are truncated. Place names in Wales may also be written with a Welsh spelling. The good news is that places given are often within the same general area of residence or birthplace. One should check the birthplace in more than one census before referring to the parish records.

For foreign-born individuals, there is sometimes an indication of British Subject, Naturalised British Subject, or Foreign Subject. Instructions on how and when to use these terms were not always clearly understood. As always you should use other records to confirm any leads obtained from the census.

PHYSICAL AND MENTAL CONDITION

Starting in 1851, the final column on census forms indicates physical and mental condition. The 1851 and 1861 censuses inquired whether a person was blind, deaf, or dumb. In 1871, the categories of imbecile, idiot, and lunatic were added. The definition of each of the terms used was not exceptionally clear, and answers reflect the vagueness of the instructions as well as the individual interpretations applied. The information in this column should be regarded with some caution since few people were willing to declare a family member an "idiot." In 1901, the term "idiot" was traded for the less harsh term "feeble minded," and the number of people recorded in this category rose significantly.[1]

Check all census years even if you think you know everything about your family, you may find a surprise. Compare the information you find in the census with

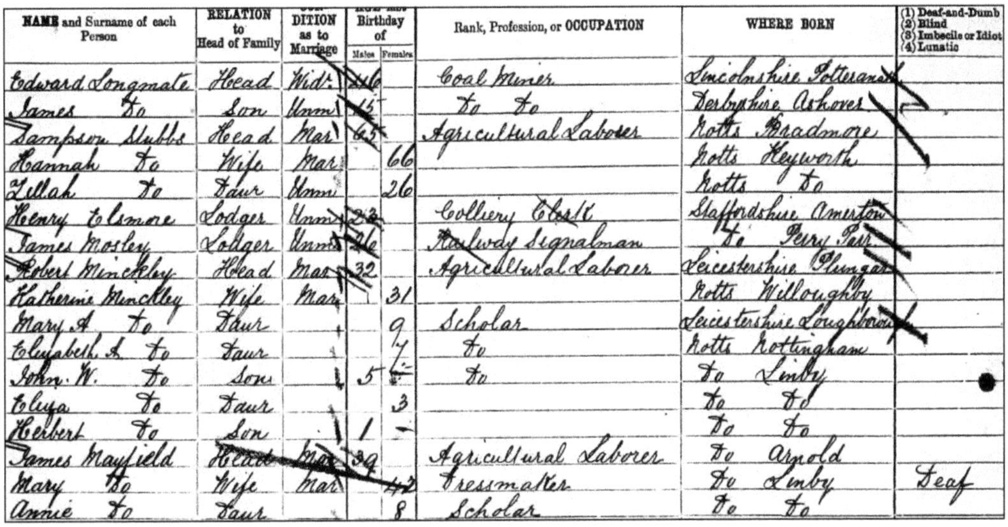

NAME and Surname of each Person	RELATION to Head of Family	DITION as to Marriage	Birthday of Males	Birthday of Females	Rank, Profession, or OCCUPATION	WHERE BORN	(1) Deaf-and-Dumb (2) Blind (3) Imbecile or Idiot (4) Lunatic
Edward Longmate	Head	Wid	66		Coal Miner	Lincolnshire Potterand	
James Do	Son	Unm	15		Do Do	Derbyshire Ashover	
Sampson Stubbs	Head	Mar	65		Agricultural Laborer	Notts Bradmore	
Hannah Do	Wife	Mar		66		Notts Heyworth	
Zillah Do	Daur	Unm		26		Notts Do	
Henry Elsmore	Lodger	Unm	23		Colliery Clerk	Staffordshire Amerton	
James Mosley	Lodger	Unm	26		Railway Signalman	Do Perry Barr	
Robert Minckley	Head	Mar	32		Agricultural Laborer	Leicestershire Plungar	
Katherine Minckley	Wife	Mar		31		Notts Willoughby	
Mary A Do	Daur			9	Scholar	Leicestershire Loughborough	
Elizabeth A Do	Daur			7	Do	Notts Nottingham	
John W. Do	Son		5		Do	Do Linby	
Eliza Do	Daur			3		Do Do	
Herbert Do	Son		1			Do Do	
James Mayfield	Head	Mar	39		Agricultural Laborer	Do Arnold	
Mary Do	Wife	Mar		42	Dressmaker	Do Linby	Deaf
Annie Do	Daur			8	Scholar	Do Do	

Figure 6.2. Portion of a return showing a woman as deaf in 1881 (RG11\3337, f.87, p.6).

information you know from other records and from other census years. Many inaccurate answers can be weeded out by taking the most common and persistent information from various records.

Using the census, or any record in family history research, is a continual cycle. First you decide what you are looking for, then you locate and analyze the record, and then compare it to other information to see what agrees and disagrees, which will lead you to another record, and you start the cycle all over again.

CASE STUDY—INTERPRETING THE RECORDS

In this example, I will show a part of my experiences as I tried to locate the parents of one of my ancestors with the help of census records.

My goal was to find the parents of my fourth great-grandfather William Mayfield. I began by examining the various records I had for the William Mayfield family. Those records showed the family as follows:

William Mayfield (b. abt. 1807) = Ann Holmes (b. abt. 1806)

    Hannah Mayfield, b. 10 Jan 1825

    Rebecca Mayfield, b. 8 Jul 1826

    Ann Mayfield, b. 6 Jul 1831

    Mark Mayfield, chr. 13 Apr 1834

    George Mayfield, chr. 26 Nov 1837

    Elizabeth Mayfield, b. 30 May 1839

    James Mayfield, b. 28 Jan 1842

    Mary Mayfield, b. 29 Jul 1845

    George Mayfield, b. 1 Mar 1848

    Sarah Mayfield, b. 28 Jan 1852

All family records indicated that the Mayfield family lived in Arnold, Nottingham. My main interest was to see what I could learn about the parents of William Mayfield. Since William married in 1824, I did not expect to find his parents actually living with him in any of the census records, unless they were quite elderly, but I believed the census could still help me make a connection.

William Mayfield died in 1890, so the first census I could find him in was 1881. Working from the known to the unknown, I planned to find him in 1881 and then work my way back to the 1841 census. Because there weren't extensive indexes online at the time, I used the method shown in chapter 5 and determined that the only finding aids available for the Arnold parish were the surname and place indexes for 1881.

Finding the Mayfield family in 1881 was a simple task of locating them on the correct microfiche index. For the other census years, I located the film I needed by looking up the parish of Arnold in the *Census Guide* and acquiring all of the micro-film numbers that I needed to view the census records at the Family History Library. Since Arnold is a small place, I was able to locate the family in all other census years by scrolling through the parish page by page. Because I was looking at every page anyway, I decided that I would record all of the census records for any family with the surname Mayfield.

In the 1881 census, I located the family of William Mayfield in Arnold, where William and Ann were living with two grandchildren. William's occupation was given as Frame Work Knitter (RG11\3336, f.42, p.29). In 1871 the family resided in Arnold and included two children and four grandchildren (RG10\3492, f.42, p.32). Six of the Mayfield children are enumerated alongside their parents in 1861 (RG9\2443, F.38, p.22).

In 1851 the enumerator recorded the surname of the family as Mafield (HO107\2128, f.197, p.34). I'm sure I have the correct family, because it includes wife Ann and children Eliza (probably Elizabeth), age 11; James, age 9; Mary, age 5; and George, age 3. William is still listed as a Framework Knitter.

By the time I got back to 1841, I was feeling confident that William Mayfield was a Framework knitter who lived his entire life in the parish of Arnold, Nottinghamshire. His birthplace is recorded as Arnold on all of the census returns, and his age consistently puts his estimated birth date around 1807.

As I worked my way back through the years, I found lots of interesting information that fueled many other research trips, but I never found a census where William Mayfield was living with his parents. I continued to search the census until I had located every member of the family in every census year. This approach provided the breakthrough I was looking for.

In all of my census research, I had not yet seen William Mayfield's two oldest children, Hannah (born about 1825) and Rebecca (born about 1826), living with the family. I figured that there were three most likely scenarios: they passed away before the census, they lived or worked away from home, or they were married.

Since the last known record I had for these individuals was their birth record, I decided to start with the census year closest in time to those known dates. The girls would have been about fifteen at the time of the 1841 census. Marriage seemed an unlikely, although possible, option. The girls were old enough to be working outside of the home, and this seemed like a more likely situation.

Since I had been transcribing information for all of the Mayfield families in the parish, it was easy to review my notes without going back to the film. In the 1841 census, I found one Rebecca Mayfield, listed as age thirteen, living in Arnold with a Mark and Elizabeth Mayfield (HO 107/855/2, f.32, p.14). The age was close to the age

I expected for Rebecca, and since Mark and Elizabeth were in their sixties, it seemed more likely that they were Rebecca's grandparents than parents. This was exciting! But before I could come to any conclusions, I needed more information.

Following my theory, I located the family of Mark Mayfield in the 1851 census. According to the census the residents in his home were as follows:

Name	Relationship	Marital Status	Age	Occupation	Birthplace
Mark Mafield	Head	Mar	61	Framework Knitter	Notts Arnold
Elizth Mafield	Wife	Mar	62	Framework Knitter wife,	Notts Arnold
Rebc Mafield	Grandaur	U	22	Framework Knitter	Notts Arnold
Ann Mafield	Grandaur	U	19	Framework Knitter	Notts Arnold

(Source: HO 107/2128, f.195, p.31)

Again, Rebecca Mayfield was about the right age to be William's daughter, and this census clearly states that Rebecca Mayfield is Mark Mayfield's granddaughter. She is also the only Rebecca in the parish. Also, the other granddaughter, Ann Mayfield, looked like she could be the daughter that was living with William Mayfield in 1841, but was absent from the family in 1851. When I added in the knowledge that Mark was an unusual name for that area and that William had a son named Mark, I felt sure that I had found the parents of William Mayfield.

I pursued my theory through other sources where I found evidence that reinforced my conclusion that William Mayfield's father was Mark Mayfield. The census did not provide absolute proof by itself, but because families are listed together with names and relationships, I was able to get the information I needed to start down the right path.

NOTES
1. Higgs, Making Sense of the Census, 75.

Researching Individual Census Years

While general statements apply to all of the census returns, each year does have unique qualities. The available returns range from pure statistical information in 1801 to the 1901 census, which yields more personal information interesting to the family historian. It is helpful to know what questions can be answered on a census-by-census level.

Following is a summary of each census year available to the public, starting with 1801, and some statements regarding what can be expected from that census year, potential problems specific to that year, and research tips.

1801–1831

The 1801 through 1831 censuses were taken on the following dates:

- 1801—10 March
- 1811—27 May
- 1821—28 May
- 1831—30 May

There are no surviving nation-wide censuses for these years, but there are enumerator's returns for over 700 individual parishes scattered around the country. There are also census-like listings for separate places from the eighteenth century back to 1522. Details about censuses before 1841 can be found in Chapman's *Pre-1841 Censuses and Population Listings in the British Isles*, Gibson and Medlycott's *Local Census Listings: 1522–1930, Holdings in the British Isles*, or Johnson's *Census Records for Scottish Families at Home and Abroad*.

1841 CENSUS

The 1841 census was taken on the night of June 6–7. The questions on this census, and all following years, were addressed to all people residing in the house that night, plus night workers who would return in the morning. Registration Districts were the same as those used by the Registrar General.

QUESTIONS ASKED IN THE 1841 CENSUS

The 1841 census form included columns for the following:
- place of residence
- whether the house was inhabited
- names of all individuals
- age
- sex
- occupation
- whether born in the same county as enumerated in
- whether born in Foreign Country (Depending on country, returns were marked as England, Scotland, Ireland, or Foreign Parts; marked as E, S, I, or F.)

TIPS AND FACTS ABOUT THE 1841 CENSUS

The TNA record group for the 1841 census of England, Wales, the Isle of Man, and the Channel Islands is HO 107, pieces 1 to 1465. This is the only census year to use books as part of the TNA reference number.

The recorded age was rounded down to the nearest five for persons older than fifteen. For example, someone who was age twenty to twenty-four would have been recorded as being twenty years old. A person age twenty-five to twenty-nine would have been recorded as being twenty-five years old.

It is rare for middle names to be written in full, if at all.

The books are made up of up to five preliminary pages, the enumeration pages, and three pages following the nominal pages for summary information. Each page has twenty-five lines for names. Original paper forms are approximately 13" h x 8" w.

Most of the census returns were written in pencil, which can make this census difficult to read.

1851 CENSUS

The 1851 census was taken on the night of March 30–31. The questions on the census were addressed to all people residing in the house that night, plus night workers who would return in the morning. This census was the first to ask for specific relationships between people living together.

QUESTIONS ASKED IN THE 1851 CENSUS

The form used in 1851 called for the following:

- number of inhabited houses
- number of houses being built
- number of houses uninhabited
- order of enumeration
- name of street, place, or road and name or number of house
- name of all persons who slept in the home census night
- relationship to head of family
- marital condition (M, U, or W)
- age in years
- sex
- occupation
- where born (parish and county in Great Britain, country only if abroad)
- whether blind or deaf-and-dumb

TIPS AND FACTS ABOUT THE 1851 CENSUS

The TNA record group for the 1851 census of England, Wales, the Isle of Man, and the Channel Islands is HO 107, pieces 1466 to 2531.

This is the only year of the Scottish census where the census reference numbers do not match the parish number. The parish name should be included in the citation for clarity.

The CEBs are made up of seven preliminary pages and the nominal pages. Each page has twenty lines for names. Original paper forms are approximately 8" h x 12" w.

The replies to this census are mostly written in pen, which makes them more legible than 1841. However, the replies were written on blue paper, which didn't film well.

Special religious schedules were distributed to churches in 1851. This special census asked questions about weekly attendance and other statistics for each denomination. These returns are available on microfilm at both The National Archives and at the Family History Library. Many of these returns have been printed and are available by county for England and as a whole for Wales. These returns can be useful in determining which nonconformist chapels were in a given area and how popular they were with the public. This information may help you locate non-conformist ancestors.

The returns from the Manchester area have been heavily damaged by water. The Manchester and Lancashire Family History Society has spent considerable effort to recover about 180,000 names from these pages. Their index is available on CD and can be ordered from the book shop at <www.mlfhs.org.uk>.

1861 CENSUS

In 1861, the census was taken on the night of April 7–8. The questions on the census were addressed to all people residing in the house that night, plus night workers who would return in the morning.

QUESTIONS

The form used in 1861 called for the following:
- order of enumeration
- name of street, place, or road and name or number of house
- number of inhabited houses
- number of houses uninhabited
- number of houses being built
- name of all persons who slept in the home census night
- relationship to head of family
- marital condition (M, U, or W)
- age in years
- sex
- occupation
- where born (parish and county in Great Britain, country only if abroad)
- whether blind or deaf-and-dumb

The Scotland census asked an additional question about the number of rooms with one or more windows.

TIPS AND FACTS ABOUT THE 1861 CENSUS

The TNA record group for the 1861 census of England, Wales, the Isle of Man and the Channel Islands is RG 9. The census in 1861 was the first to provide separate forms for the Royal Navy and other individuals aboard ships. The number of individuals required for an institution to be counted separately was reduced to one hundred.

The microfilm copy at the Family History Library is on 16mm, and the smaller size can make it difficult to read. In addition, it was filmed backwards, which can be confusing.

The CEBs are made up of six preliminary pages and the nominal pages. Each page has twenty-five lines for name. Original paper forms are approximately 9" h x 14" w.

1871 CENSUS

The 1871 census was taken on the night of April 2–3. The questions on the census were addressed to all people residing in the house that night, plus night workers who would return in the morning.

QUESTIONS

The form used in 1871 called for the following:

- order of enumeration
- name of street, place, or road and name or number of house
- number of inhabited houses
- number of houses uninhabited
- number of houses being built
- name of all persons who slept in the home census night
- relationship to head of family
- marital condition (M, U, or W)
- age in years
- sex
- occupation
- where born (parish and county in Great Britain, country only if abroad)
- whether deaf-and-dumb, blind, imbecile or idiot, or lunatic.

The Scotland census asked an additional question about the number of rooms with one or more windows.

TIPS AND FACTS ABOUT THE 1871 CENSUS

The TNA record group for the 1871 census of England, Wales, the Isle of Man, and the Channel Islands is RG 10. There are separate forms for ships and the Royal Navy.

The CEBs are made up of six preliminary pages and the nominal pages. Each page has twenty-five lines for names. Original paper forms are approximately 9 1/2" h x 15" w.

1881 CENSUS

The census of 1881 was taken on the night of April 3–4. The questions on the census were addressed to all people residing in the house that night, plus night workers who would return in the morning.

QUESTIONS

The form used in 1881 called for the following:

- order of enumeration
- name of street, place, or road and name or number of house
- number of inhabited houses
- number of houses uninhabited
- number of houses being built
- name of all persons who slept in the home census night
- relationship to head of family

- marital condition (M, U, or W)
- age in years
- sex
- occupation
- where born (parish and county in Great Britain, country only if abroad)
- whether deaf-and-dumb, blind, imbecile or idiot, or lunatic

The Scotland census asked an additional question about the number of rooms with one or more windows.

TIPS AND FACTS ABOUT THE 1881 CENSUS

The TNA record group for the 1881 census of England, Wales, the Isle of Man, and the Channel Islands is RG 11. Separate forms were provided for institutions, ships, and the Royal Navy.

The CEBs are made up of six preliminary pages and the nominal pages. Each page has twenty-five lines for names. Original paper forms are approximately 9" h x 15" w.

1891 CENSUS

The census of 1891 was taken on the night of April 5–6. The questions on the census were addressed to all people residing in the house that night, plus night workers who would return in the morning.

QUESTIONS

The form used in 1891 called for the following:

- order of enumeration
- name of street, place, or road and name or number of house
- number of inhabited houses
- number of houses uninhabited
- number of houses being built
- number of rooms occupied if less than five
- name of all persons who slept in the home census night
- relationship to head of family
- marital condition (M, U, or W)
- age in years
- sex
- occupation
- whether employer, employed, or neither
- where born (parish and county in Great Britain, country only if abroad)
- whether deaf-and-dumb, blind, lunatic, imbecile, or idiot
- language spoken (in Wales and Scotland).

The Scotland census asked an additional question about the number of rooms with one or more windows.

TIPS AND FACTS ABOUT THE 1891 CENSUS

The TNA record group for the 1891 census of England, Wales, the Isle of Man, and the Channel Islands is RG 12. Separate forms were provided for institutions, ships, and the Royal Navy.

The CEBs are made up of six preliminary pages and the nominal pages. Each page has thirty-one lines for names. Original paper forms are approximately 11" h x 16" w.

This is the first census where women were allowed to apply to be enumerators.

1901 CENSUS

The census of 1901 was taken on the night of March 31–April 1. The questions on the census were addressed to all people residing in the house that night, plus night workers who would return in the morning. This is the most recent census available to the public.

QUESTIONS

The form used in 1901 called for the following:

- order of enumeration
- name of street, place, or road and name or number of house
- number of inhabited houses
- number of houses uninhabited (whether or not occupied)
- number of houses being built
- number of rooms occupied if less than five
- name of all persons who slept in the home census night
- relationship to head of family
- marital condition (M, U, or W)
- age in years
- sex
- occupation
- employer, worker, or own account
- whether working from home
- where born (parish and county in Great Britain, country only if abroad)
- whether deaf-and-dumb, blind, lunatic, imbecile, or feeble-minded
- language spoken (in Wales and Scotland).

The Scotland census asked an additional question about the number of rooms with one or more windows.

TIPS AND FACTS ABOUT THE 1901 CENSUS

The TNA record group for the 1901 census of England, Wales, the Isle of Man, and the Channel Islands is RG 13. Separate forms were provided for institutions, ships, and the Royal Navy.

The CEBs are made up of six preliminary pages and the nominal pages. Each page has thirty-one lines for names. Original paper forms are approximately 12" h x 17" w.

1911–2001

The 1911 through 2001 census returns are not yet available to the public. Each year will be available in January of the 101st year following the census. Unfortunately, the 1931 census returns were destroyed during World War II. The census dates for these years are as follows:

- 1911—2 April
- 1921—19 June
- 1931—26 April
- 1941—Not Taken
- 1951—8 April
- 1961—23 April
- 1971—25 April
- 1981—5 April
- 1991—21 April
- 2001—29 April

8

Census in Ireland

Due to its physical proximity, and the frequent migration of people to and from Ireland, it is worth discussing the basics of the census in Ireland. The first census in Ireland took place in 1813. The next census was taken in 1821, and every ten years thereafter until 1911. Due to civil war, the next census was not until 1926 and then again in 1936. From 1946 to 1971 censuses were taken every five years. Since 1971, a census has been taken every ten years.

The census of 1813 no longer exists. Most of the returns from 1821 to 1851 were destroyed in a fire. The government destroyed all of the returns from 1861 to 1891 once the statistical information had been compiled. The censuses of 1901 and 1911 are archived at the National Archives in Dublin.

The National Archives
Bishop Street
Dublin 8
Ireland
Tel: 353 (1) 407 2300
Fax: 353 (1) 407 2333
E-mail: mail@nationalarchives.ie
URL: www.nationalarchives.ie

The remaining censuses are not yet available to the public.

The questions asked on the Irish census are different than those on the censuses for England, Wales, and Scotland. For the surviving censuses of 1821 to 1851, the only one that did not request individual information for every member of the house is 1831. All of the others asked about each individual and include questions regarding name, age, occupation, and relationship to the head of the house. In 1841 and 1851, the marital status, sex, and birthplace was also recorded.

In 1851, two additional forms were available. One was for absent members of the house and the other was for members of the household that had died since the last census. The latter form is valuable as it records date of and age at death for those individuals.

The 1901 and 1911 censuses asked about name, age, sex, relationship to the head of the house, religion, occupation, marital status, county of birth (except for foreign births, which give country only), whether the individual spoke Irish, and whether the individual could read or write. The 1911 census also had questions for married women, including the number of years she had been married to her current husband, the number of children that had been born to them, and the number of their children who were still alive.

Table 8.1 Chapman Codes for Ireland

Ireland (IRL)

ANT	Antrim	LIM	Limerick
ARM	Armagh	LDY	Londonderry
CAR	Carlow	LOG	Longford
CAV	Cavan	LOU	Louth
CLA	Clare	MAY	Mayo
COR	Cork	MEA	Meath
DON	Donegal	MOG	Monaghan
DOW	Down	OFF	Offaly
DUB	Dublin	ROS	Roscommon
FER	Fermanagh	SLI	Sligo
GAL	Galway	TIP	Tipperary
KER	Kerry	TYR	Tyrone
KID	Kildare	WAT	Waterford
KIK	Kilkenny	WEM	Westmeath
LET	Leitrim	WEX	Wexford
LEX	Leix	WIC	Wicklow

A more detailed examination of the census of Ireland, and Irish records in general, can be found in *Finding Your Irish Ancestors: A Beginner's Guide*, by David Ouimette (Ancestry, 2005).

Appendix A: Glossary

abstract of totals

A page in the *Census Enumerator's Book* that contains a statistical breakdown of the numbers of people and buildings within each *enumeration district*.

British Isles

Term used to refer to all of England, Wales, Scotland, Northern Ireland, the Republic of Ireland, the Channel Islands, and the Isle of Man.

census

A census is a counting, or enumeration, and description of a population. What percentage of the population to count and what questions to ask are determined by the purpose of the census. Most modern censuses take place at regular intervals, such as every ten years.

Census Enumerator's Book

Book where the enumerator compiled all the information gathered from individual Householder's Schedules. Sometimes referred to as a "CEB."

civil parish

A local administrative unit. Many started out as tithings or hamlets and, after the introduction of the Poor Law 1866, acquired the name *parish*.

civil registration

National registration of births, marriages, deaths, and divorces.

county

In general use, the term usually referring to ancient or geographic counties. Ancient counties are counties that were established before 1066. Poor law unions, established in 1834, could include parishes from multiple ancient counties. The registrar general created administrative counties for the census that are roughly based on these poor law unions. Registration or administrative counties are not always the same as an ancient county though they may have the same name.

County Record Office (CRO) — Home of records for a *county* or district.

declaration sheet — A page in the *Census Enumerator's Book* containing signed declarations of accuracy by the individuals responsible for the *enumeration district* that follows in the census returns.

ecclesiastical parish — An administrative unit used by a church or religious group. A division used by both the Church of England and the Church of Scotland.

enumeration district — An area within a *registration sub-district* with specific boundaries based on population. The basic unit by which the census returns are arranged. Also called an "E.D."

enumeration page — A page in the *Census Enumerator's Book,* copied from the household schedules, that contains personal information for each person enumerated. Also called a nominal page.

enumerator — A person who delivered and collected household schedules, assisted with their completion, and then copied out the information into the *Census Enumerator's Book.*

example page — A pre-printed *enumeration page* in the *Census Enumerator's Book* showing how the *enumerator* should complete the forms.

Federation of Family History Societies (FFHS) — The umbrella organization for family history societies mainly in England and Wales, but with many associate members overseas.

Family History Center	Local branch of the Family History Library in Salt Lake City, Utah, operated by The Church of Jesus Christ of Latter-day Saints.
family history society	A society, often non-profit, made up of individuals interested in researching, sharing, and preserving genealogy and family history, usually for a specific region or name.
folio	A stamped number that refers to two sides of a *page*; part of the TNA reference number.
Great Britain	Term used to refer to the countries of England, Wales, and Scotland.
hamlet	The smallest of population centers. A hamlet is often not large enough to possess a church, inn, public house, or other community facilities.
institution	Any establishment such as a hospital, asylum, work-house, school, prison, or so on.
instruction sheet	A pre-printed document of instructions in the *Census Enumerator's Book* that explains how *enumerators* should complete the *census*.
nominal page	See *Enumeration Page*.
Office of National Statistics	Government organization in the United Kingdom that is responsible for collecting and producing economic and social statistics. The survey and records they keep to produce these statistics are often very valuable to genealogists.
Old Parish Registers (OPR)	When civil registration began in Scotland in 1855, the Old Parish Registers of the Established Church of Scotland were put in to the care of the Registrar General's Office. Each *parish* is assigned a unique reference number that is used in many record collections.
page	Page numbers pre-printed on census forms starting over with page one in each *enumeration district*.

parish	A type of administrative unit for either civil government or church administration.
piece	A bundle of *Census Enumerator's Book*s. Part of the TNA reference number.
Public Records Office (PRO)	In 2003, the PRO joined with the Historical Manuscripts Commission to become The National Archives.
registration district	Established in 1837 and based on poor law union areas. England and Wales were divided into a number of districts for the purposes of registering births, deaths, marriages, and census returns. The name of each registration district can be found on the Description of Enumeration District page. Registration districts often contained civil parishes from more than one county.
registration sub-district	Subdivision of a *registration district* with specified boundaries.
schedule number	A number given to each distinct household within an *enumeration district*.
summary of civil parishes	A page containing a statistical summary of the numbers of people and buildings within each *enumeration district*.
town	Population is not the only factor, but a town is usually an area of mid-size population, between 1,500 and 5,000. The term is often applied to *villages* and *hamlets* as well as cities or boroughs. A town often has an ancient regular market and a definite commercial area.
township	Subdivision of *parish*—usually for poor law purposes.
United Kingdom	The full term is the United Kingdom of Great Britain and Northern Ireland. Used to refer to all of England, Wales, Scotland, and Northern Ireland. When the term is used before 1921, it includes

all of Ireland. To include the Republic of Ireland use the term *British Isles.* The Isle of Man and the Channel Islands are often grouped with the United Kingdom, although they are mostly self-governed and not legally part of the United Kingdom.

village Subdivision of a *parish,* normally with a small population.

Appendix B: Addresses to Libraries and Archives

CHANNEL ISLANDS

JERSEY
Jersey Archive
Clarence Road
St. Helier
Jersey
JE2 4JY

GUERNSEY
The Priaulx Library
Candie
St. Peter Port
Guernsey
GY1 1UG
Tel: 01481 721 998
Fax: 01481 713 804
E-mail: priaulx.library@gov.gg
URL: www.priaulx.gov.gg

ENGLAND

THE NATIONAL ARCHIVES
Kew, Richmond, Surrey,
TW9 4DU
United Kingdom
www.nationalarchives.gov.uk

FAMILY RECORDS CENTRE
1 Myddelton Street

London EC1R 1UW
United Kingdom
www.familyrecords.gov.uk/frc

COUNTY RECORD OFFICES
AND OTHER ARCHIVES

BEDFORDSHIRE
Bedfordshire and Luton Records and
Archives Service
Riverside Building
County Hall
Cauldwell Street
Bedford
MK42 9AP
Tel: 01234 228 833/228 777
Fax: 01234 228 854
E-mail: archive@bedscc.gov.uk
URL: www.bedfordshire.gov.uk/archive

BERKSHIRE
Berkshire Record Office
9 Coley Avenue
Reading
Berks
RG1 6AF
Tel: 0118 901 5132
Fax: 0118 901 5131
E-mail: arch@reading.gov.uk
URL: www.berkshirerecordoffice.org.uk

BUCKINGHAMSHIRE
Centre for Buckinghamshire Studies
County Hall
Walton Street
Aylesbury
HP20 1UU
Tel: 01296 382 587
E-mail: archives@buckscc.gov.uk
URL: www.buckscc.gov.uk/archives/
index.stm

CAMBRIDGESHIRE
County Record Office Cambridge
Shire Hall
Castle Hill
Cambridge
CB3 0AP
Tel: 01223 717 281
Fax: 01223 717 201
E-mail: County.Records.Cambridge@
cambridgeshire.gov.uk
URL: www.cambridgeshire.gov.uk/lei-
sure/archives/visiting/crocambridge.htm

CHESHIRE
Cheshire Record Office
Duke Street
Chester
CH1 1RL
Tel: 01244 602 574
E-mail: recordoffice@cheshire.gov.uk.
URL: www.cheshire.gov.uk/recoff/
home.htm

CORNWALL
Cornwall Record Office
Old County Hall
Truro
Cornwall
TR1 3AY
Tel: 01872 323 127
Fax: 01872 322 292
E-mail: cro@cornwall.gov.uk
URL: www.cornwall.gov.uk/index.
cfm?articleid=307

CUMBERLAND
Cumbria Record Office and Local

Studies Library, Barrow
140 Duke Street
Barrow-in-Furness
Cumbria
LA14 1XW
Tel: 01229 894 363
Fax: 01229 894 364
E-mail: barrow.record.office@cumbriacc.
gov.uk
URL: www.cumbria.gov.uk/archives

Cumbria Record Office, Carlisle
The Castle
Carlisle
Cumbria
CA3 8UR
Tel: 01228 607 285/607 284
Fax: 01228 707 274
E-mail: hetland.record.office@cumbri-
acc.gov.uk
URL: www.cumbria.gov.uk/archives

Cumbria Record Office, Kendal
Kendal County Offices
Kendal
Cumbria
LA9 4RQ
Tel: 01539 773 540 or 773 539
Fax: 01539 773 538
E-mail: hetla.record.office@cumbriacc.
gov.uk
URL: www.cumbria.gov.uk/archives

Cumbria Record Office and
Local Studies Library, Whitehaven
Scotch Street
Whitehaven
Cumbria
CA28 7NL
Tel: 01946 852 920
Fax: 01946 852 919
E-mail: hetlandh.record.office@cumbri-
acc.gov.uk
URL: www.cumbria.gov.uk/archives

DERBYSHIRE
Derbyshire Record Office

County Hall
Matlock
Derbyshire
DE4 3AG
Tel: 01629 585 347
Fax: 01629 576 11
E-mail: record.office@derbyshire.gov.uk
URL: www.derbyshire.gov.uk/record-office

DEVON
Devon Record Office
Great Moor House
Bittern Road
Sowton
Exeter
Devon
EX2 7NL
Tel: 01392 384 253
Fax: 01392 384 256
E-mail: devrec@devon.gov.uk
URL: www.devon.gov.uk/record_office.htm

North Devon Record Office
Library and Record Office
Tuly Street
Barnstaple
EX31 1EL
Tel: 01271 388 607
Fax: 01271 388 608
E-mail: ndevrec@devon.gov.uk
URL: www.devon.gov.uk/record_office.htm

Plymouth and West Devon Record
Office
Unit 3
Clare Place
Plymouth
PL4 0JW
Tel: 01752 305 940
E-mail: pwdro@plymouth.gov.uk
URL: www.plymouth.gov.uk/archives

DORSET
Dorset History Centre

Bridport Road
Dorchester
DT1 1RP
Tel: 01305 250 550
Fax: 01305 257 184
E-mail: archives@dorsetcc.gov.uk
URL: www.dorsetcc.gov.uk/index.jsp?articleid=2203

DURHAM
Durham Record office
County Hall
DH1 5UL
Tel: 0191 383 3253
Fax: 0191 383 4500
E-mail: record.office@durham.gov.uk
URL: www.durham.gov.uk/recordoffice

ESSEX
Essex Record Office
Wharf Road
Chelmsford
CM2 6YT
Tel: 01245 244 644
Fax: 01245 244 655
E-mail: ero.enquiry@essexcc.gov.uk
URL: www.essexcc.gov.uk/vip8/ecc/ECCWebsite/display/guides/ero_guide_guide_119186_ArchivesAndMuseums/index.jsp

COLCHESTER & NORTH EAST ESSEX BRANCH
Stanwell House
Stanwell St
Colchester
Essex
CO2 7DL
Tel: 01206 572 099
Fax: 01206 574 541
E-mail: ero.colchester@essexcc.gov.uk
URL: www.essexcc.gov.uk/vip8/ecc/ECCWebsite/display/guides/ero_guide_guide_119186_ArchivesAndMuseums/index.jsp

SOUTHEND BRANCH
Central Library
Victoria Ave
Southend-on-Sea
SS2 6EX
Tel: 01702 612 621 Ext 215
E-mail: ero.southend@essexcc.gov.uk
URL: www.essexcc.gov.uk/vip8/ecc/
ECCWebsite/display/guides/ero_guide_
guide_119186_ArchivesAndMuseums/
index.jsp

GLOUCESTERSHIRE
Gloucestershire Record Office
Clarence Row
Alvin Street
Gloucester
GL1 3DW
Tel: 01452 425 295
Fax: 01452 426 378
E-mail: records@gloucestershire.gov.uk
URL: www.gloucestershire.gov.uk/
index.cfm?articleid=1348

BRISTOL RECORD OFFICE
"B" Bond Warehouse
Smeaton Road
Bristol
BS1 6XN
Tel: 0117 922 4224
Fax: 0117 922 4236
E-mail: bro@bristol-city.gov.uk
URL: www.bristol-city.gov.uk/ccm/
content/Leisure-Culture/Local-History-
Heritage/Bristol-Record-Office-pages/
bristol-record-office.en

HAMPSHIRE
Hampshire Record Office
Sussex Street
Winchester
SO23 8TH
Tel: 01962 846 154
E-mail: enquiries.archives@hants.gov.uk
URL: www.hants.gov.uk/record-office/
index.html

ISLE OF WIGHT RECORD OFFICE
26 Hillside
Newport
PO30 2EB
Tel: 01983 823 820 or 01983 823 821
Fax: 01983 823 820
E-mail: record.office@iow.gov.uk
URL: www.iwight.com/library/record_
office/default.asp

HEREFORDSHIRE
Herefordshire Record Office
Harold Street
Hereford
HR1 2QX
Tel: 01432 260 750
Fax: 01432 260 066
E-mail: archives@herefordshire.gov.uk
URL: www.herefordshire.gov.uk/leisure/
libraries/3584.asp

See also the *Worcestershire, WorcesterLibrary
and History Centre*

HERTFORDSHIRE
Hertfordshire Record Office
County Hall
Pegs Lane
Hertford
SG13 8DE
Tel: 01438 737 333

HUNTINGDONSHIRE
County Record Office Huntingdon
Grammar School Walk
Huntingdon
PE29 6LF
Tel: 01480 375 842
Fax: 01480 375 842
E-mail: county.records.hunts@cam-
bridgeshire.gov.uk
URL: www.cambridgeshire.gov.uk/
leisure/archives/visiting/crohuntingdon.
htm

See also the *Cambridgeshire, County
Record Office Cambridge*

KENT
The Centre for Kentish Studies
Sessions House
County Hall
Maidstone
Kent
ME14 1XQ
Tel: 01622 694 363
Fax: 01622 694 379
E-mail: archives@kent.gov.uk
URL: www.kent.gov.uk/leisure-and-culture/archives-and-local-history/archive-centres/centre-for-kentish-studies.htm

EAST KENT ARCHIVES CENTRE
Enterprise Zone
Honeywood Road
Whitfield, Dover
CT16 3EH.
Tel: 01304 829 306
E-mail: eastkentarchives@kent.gov.uk
URL: www.kent.gov.uk/leisure-and-culture/archives-and-local-history/archive-centres/east-kent-archives-centre.htm

LANCASHIRE
Lancashire Record Office
Bow Lane
Preston
Lancashire
PR1 2RE
Tel: 01772 533 039
Fax: 01772 533 050
E-mail: Record.Office@ed.lancscc.gov.uk
URL: www.lancashire.gov.uk/education/record_office

LIVERPOOL RECORD OFFICE
Central Library
William Brown Street
Liverpool
L3 8EW
Tel: 0151 233 5817
Fax: 0151 233 5886
E-mail: recoffice.central.library@liverpool.gov.uk
URL: http://archive.liverpool.gov.uk

See also *Cumberland, Cumbria Record Office and Local Studies Library, Barrow*

LEICESTERSHIRE
Leicestershire Record Office
Long Street
Wigston Magna
Leicester
LE18 2AH
Tel: 0116 257 1080
Fax: 0116 257 1120
E-mail: recordoffice@leics.gov.uk
URL: www.leics.gov.uk/index/community/museums/record_office.htm

LINCOLNSHIRE
Lincolnshire Archives
St. Rumbold Street
Lincoln
Lincolnshire
LN2 5AB
Tel: 01522 525 158
Fax: 01522 530 047
E-mail: Archive@lincolnshire.gov.uk
URL: www.lincolnshire.gov.uk/index.asp?docId=34806

North East Lincolnshire Archives
(Humberside)
Grimsby Town Hall
Grimsby
Lincolnshire
DN31 1HX
Tel: 01472 323 585
Fax: 01472 323 582
E-mail: Archivist@nelincs.gov.uk
URL: www.nelincs.gov.uk

LONDON
London Metropolitan Archives
40 Northampton Road
London
EC1R 0HB
Tel: 020 7332 3820

Fax: 020 7833 9136
E-mail: ask.lma@cityoflondon.gov.uk
URL: www.cityoflondon.gov.uk/
leisure_heritage/libraries_archives_
museums_galleries/lma

GREATER MANCHESTER COUNTY RECORD OFFICE
56 Marshall Street
New Cross
Manchester
M4 5FU
Tel: 0161 832 5284
Fax: 0161 839 3808
E-mail: archives@gmcro.co.uk
URL: www.gmcro.co.uk

MIDDLESEX
See *London, London Metropolitan Archives*

NORFOLK
Norfolk Record Office
The Archive Centre
Martineau Lane
Norwich
NR1 2DQ
Tel: 01603 222 599
Fax: 01603 761 885
E-mail: norfrec@norfolk.gov.uk
URL: www.archives.norfolk.gov.uk/nro-index.htm

NORTHAMPTONSHIRE
Northamptonshire Record Office
Wootton Hall Park
Northampton
NN4 8BQ
Tel: 01604 762 129
Fax: 01604 767 562
E-mail: archivist@northamptonshire.gov.uk
URL: www.northamptonshire.gov.uk/
Community/record/about_us.htm

NORTHUMBERLAND
Northumberland Record Office
Melton Park

North Gosforth
Newcastle upon Tyne
NE3 5QX
Tel: 0191 236 2680
Fax: 0191 217 0905
URL: http://pscm.northum-
berland.gov.uk/portal/page?_
pageid=106,54411&_dad=portal92&_
schema=PORTAL92&pid=448

NOTTINGHAMSHIRE
Nottinghamshire Archives
County House
Castle Meadow Road
Nottingham
NG2 1AG
Tel: 0115 958 1634
Fax: 0115 941 3997
E-mail: archives@nottscc.gov.uk
URL: www.nottscc.gov.uk/libraries/
Archives

OXFORDSHIRE
Oxfordshire Record Office
St Luke's Church
Temple Road
Cowley
Oxford
OX4 2HT
Tel: 01865 398 200
Fax: 01865 398 201
E-mail: archives@oxfordshire.gov.uk
URL: www.oxfordshire.gov.
uk/wps/portal/publicsite/
councilservices?WCM_GLOBAL_
CONTEXT=http://apps.oxfordshire.
gov.uk/wps/wcm/connect/Internet/
Council+Services/Leisure+and+culture/
History+and+heritage/Oxfordshire+
Record+Office

RUTLAND
See *Leicestershire, Leicestershire Record Office*

SHROPSHIRE
Shropshire Archives
Castle Gates

Shrewsbury
SY1 2AQ
Tel: 01743 255 350
Fax: 01743 255 355
E-mail: archives@shropshire-cc.gov.uk
URL: www.shropshire.gov.uk/archives.nsf

SOMERSET
Somerset Record Office
Obridge Road
Taunton
TA2 7PU
Tel: 01823 278 805
Fax: 01823 325 402
E-mail: archives@somerset.gov.uk
URL: www.somerset.gov.uk/archives

STAFFORDSHIRE
Staffordshire Record Office
Eastgate Street
Stafford
ST16 2LZ
Tel: 01785 278 379
Fax: 01785 278 384
E-mail: staffordshire.record.office@staf-
fordshire.gov.uk
URL: www.staffordshire.gov.uk/leisure/
archives

SUFFOLK
Suffolk Record Office
77 Raingate Street
Bury St Edmunds
IP33 2AR
Tel: 01284 352 352
Fax: 01284 352 355
E-mail: bury.ro@libher.suffolkcc.gov.uk
URL: www.suffolkcc.gov.uk/sro

Suffolk Record Office
Gatacre Road
Ipswich
IP1 2LQ
Tel: 01473 584 541
Fax: 01473 584 533
E-mail: Ipswich.ro@libher.suffolkcc.gov.uk
URL: www.suffolkcc.gov.uk/sro

Suffolk Record Office
Central Library
Clapham Road
Lowestoft
NR32 1DR
Tel: 01502 405 357
Fax: 01502 405 350
E-mail: lowestoft.ro@libher.suffolkcc.
gov.uk
URL: www.suffolkcc.gov.uk/sro

SURREY
Surrey History Centre
130 Goldsworth Road
Woking
Surrey
GU21 6ND
Tel: 01483 518 737
Email: shs@surreycc.gov.uk
URL: www.surreycc.gov.uk/surreyhisto-
ryservice

SUSSEX
The East Sussex Record Office
The Maltings
Castle Precincts
Lewes
East Sussex
BN7 1YT
Tel: 01273 482 349
Fax: 01273 482 341
E-mail: archives@eastsussexcc.gov.uk
URL: www.eastsussexcc.gov.uk/
leisureandtourism/localandfamilyhistory/
useourarchives

West Sussex Record Office
County Hall
Chichester
West Sussex
PO19 1RN
Tel : 01243 753 600
Fax : 01243 533 959
E-mail : records.office@westsussex.gov.uk
URL: www.westsussex.gov.uk/ccm/
navigation/libraries-and-archives/record-
office

WARWICKSHIRE
Warwickshire County Record Office
Priory Park
Cape Road
Warwick
CV34 4JS
Tel: 1926 738 959
Fax: 1926 738 969
E-mail: recordoffice@warwickshire.gov.uk
URL: www.warwickshire.gov.uk/countyrecordoffice

WESTMORLAND
See *Cumberland, Cumbria Record Office, Kendal*

WILTSHIRE
Wiltshire and Swindon Record Office
Libraries and Heritage Headquarters
Bythesea Road
Trowbridge
Wiltshire
BA14 8BS
Tel: 1225 713 138
Fax: 1225 731 515
E-mail: wsro@wiltshire.gov.uk
URL: www.wiltshire.gov.uk/heritage/html/wsro.html

WORCESTERSHIRE
Worcester Library and History Centre
Trinity Street
Worcester
WR1 2PW
Tel: 01905 765 922 / 765 924
Fax: 01905 765 925
E-mail: WLHC@worcestershire.gov.uk
URL: www.worcestershire.gov.uk/home/wccindex/wcc-records/wcc-records-history-centre.htm

See also the *Herefordshire, Herefordshire Record Office*

YORKSHIRE
East Riding
East Riding of Yorkshire Archives

Service
County Hall
Beverley
East Riding of Yorkshire
HU17 9BA
Tel: 01482 393 939
Fax: 01482 393 375
E-mail: customer.services@eastriding.gov.uk
URL: www.eastriding.gov.uk/libraries/archives/archives.html

North Riding
North Yorkshire County Record Office
Malpas Road
Northallerton
North Yorkshire
DL7 8TB
Tel: 01609 777 585
Fax: 01609 777 078
E-mail: archives@northyorks.gov.uk
URL: www.northyorks.gov.uk/public/site/NYCC/menuitem.72980bf1db3dfb9fd7428f1040008a0c/?vgnextoid=6978a6cd3facbf00VgnVCMServer0d6519acRCRD

West Riding
Wakefield Headquarters
Registry of Deeds
Newstead Road
Wakefield
WF1 2DE
Tel: 01924 305 980
Fax: 01924 305 983
E-mail: wakefield@wyjs.org.uk
URL: www.archives.wyjs.org.uk/index.htm

Bradford Archives
15 Canal Road
Bradford
BD1 4AT
Tel: 01274 731 931
Fax: 01274 734 013
E-mail: hetland@wyjs.org.uk
URL: www.archives.wyjs.org.uk/index.htm

Calderdale Archives
Central Library
Northgate House
Northgate
Halifax
HX1 1UN
Tel: 01422 392 636
Fax: 01422 341 083
E-mail: calderdale@wyjs.org.uk
URL: www.archives.wyjs.org.uk/index.
htm

Kirklees Archives
Central Library
Princess Alexandra Walk
Huddersfield
HD1 2SU
Tel: 01484 542 297
Fax: 01484 542 297
E-mail: kirklees@wyjs.org.uk
URL: www.archives.wyjs.org.uk/index.
htm

Leeds Archives
Chapeltown Road
Sheepscar
Leeds
LS7 3AP
Tel: 0113 214 5814
Fax: 0113 214 5815
URL: leeds@wyjs.org.uk
URL: www.archives.wyjs.org.uk/index.
htm

ISLE OF MAN

NATIONAL LIBRARY AND ARCHIVES
Manx National Heritage
Douglas
Isle of Man
IM1 3LY
E-mail: enquiries@mnh.gov.im
URL: www.gov.im/mnh

SCOTLAND

GENERAL REGISTER OFFICE FOR SCOTLAND
New Register House
3 West Register Street
Edinburgh
EH1 3YT
Tel: 0131 334 0380
URL: www.gro-scotland.gov.uk

Ladywell House (for census)
Edinburgh
EH12 7TF
Tel: 0131 334 0380
URL: www.gro-scotland.gov.uk

Monreith House
The Crichton
Bankend Road
Dumfries
Scotland
DG1 4ZE
Tel: 0131 334 0380
URL: www.gro-scotland.gov.uk

THE NATIONAL ARCHIVES OF SCOTLAND
H M GENERAL REGISTER HOUSE
2 Princes Street
Edinburgh
EH1 3YY
Tel: 0131 535 1334
Fax: 0131 535 1328
E-mail: enquiries@nas.gov.uk
URL: www.nas.gov.uk

COUNTY RECORD OFFICES AND OTHER ARCHIVES

ABERDEENSHIRE
Aberdeen City Archives
Town House
Broad Street
Aberdeen
AB10 1AQ
Tel: 01224 522 513
Fax: 01224 638 556

E-mail: archives@aberdeencity.gov.uk
URL: www.aberdeencity.gov.uk

Aberdeenshire Council Archives
Old Aberdeen House
Dunbar Street
Aberdeen
AB24 3UJ
Tel: 01224 481 775
Fax: 01224 495 830
E-mail: archives@aberdeencity.gov.uk
URL: www.aberdeenshire.gov.uk

Aberdeen City Library
Central Library
Rosemount Viaduct
Aberdeen
AB25 1GW
Tel: 1224 652511
Fax: 1224 624118
E-mail: ReferenceLibrary@aberdeencity.
gov.uk

ANGUS

Angus Archives
Hunter Library
Restenneth Priory
by Forfar
DD8 2SZ
Tel: 01307 468644
E-mail: angus.archives@angus.gov.uk
URL: www.angus.gov.uk/history/
archives

ARGYLL

Argyll and Bute District Libraries
Library Headquarters
Highland Avenue
Sandbank
Dunoon
PA23 8PB
Tel: 01369 703214
Fax: 01369 705797
URL: www.argyll-bute.gov.uk

AYRSHIRE

Ayrshire Archives Centre

Craigie Estate
Ayr
KA8 0SS
Tel: 01292 287 584
Fax: 01292 284 918
E-mail: archives@south-ayrshire.gov.uk
URL: www.ayrshirearchives.org.uk

BANFFSHIRE

See *General Register Office for Scotland*

BERWICKSHIRE

Scottish Borders Archive and Local
History Centre
St Mary's Mill
Selkirk
TD7 5EU
Tel: 01750 724903
Fax: 01750 22875
E-mail: archives@scotborders.gov.uk
URL: www.scottishborders.gov.uk

BUTE

Argyll and Bute District Libraries
Library Headquarters
Highland Avenue
Sandbank
Dunoon
PA23 8PB
Tel: 01369 703214
Fax: 01369 705797
URL: www.argyll-bute.gov.uk

Bute Archive at Mount Stuart
Mount Stuart House and Gardens
Rothesay
Isle of Bute
PA20 9LR
Tel: 01700 503 877
Fax: 01700 505 313
E-mail: contactus@mountstuart.com
URL: www.mountstuart.com

CAITHNESS

North Highland Archive
Wick Library
Sinclair Terrace

Wick
Caithness
KW1 5AB
Tel: 01955 606432
Fax: 01955 603000
E-mail: north.highlandarchive@high-
land.gov.uk
URL: www.highland.gov.uk/leisure/
archives/northhighlandarchive

CLACKMANNANSHIRE

Clackmannanshire Council Archives
26-28 Drysdale Street
Alloa
FK10 1JL
Tel: 01259 722 262
Fax: 01259 219 469
E-mail: libraries@clacks.gov.uk
URL: www.clacksweb.org.uk/culture/
archives

DUMFRIESSHIRE

Dumfries and Galloway Archives
Archive Centre
33 Burns Street
Dumfries
DG1 2PS
Tel: 01387 269 254
Fax: 01387 264 126
E-mail: libarchive@dumgal.gov.uk
URL: www.dumgal.gov.uk/dumgal/
Services.aspx?id=40

Ewart Library
Catherine Street
Dumfries
Dumfries
DG1 1JB
Tel: 01387 253 820 / 01387 252 070
Fax: 01387 260 294
E-mail: libs&i@dumgal.gov.uk
URL: www.dumgal.gov.uk/dumgal/
MiniWeb.aspx?id=86&menuid=980&op
enid=949

DUNBARTONSHIRE

William Patrick Library

2-4 West High Street
Kirkintilloch
G66 1AD
Tel: 0141 776 8090
Fax: 0141 776 0408
E-mail: libraries@eastdunbarton.gov.uk
URL: www.eastdunbarton.gov.uk

EAST LOTHIAN

Local History Centre
Haddington Library
Newton Port
Haddington
EH41 3HA
Tel: 01620 823 307
E-mail: localhistory@eastlothian.gov.uk
URL: www.eastlothian.gov.uk/
content/0,1094,1485,00.html

EDINBURGH

Edinburgh City Archives
City Chambers
High Street
Edinburgh
EH1 1YJ
Tel: 0131 529 4616
Fax: 0131 529 4957
URL: www.edinburgh.gov.uk

FIFE

Fife Council Archive Centre
Carleton House
Balgonie Road
Markinch
KY7 6AQ
Tel: 01592 416 504
E-mail: hetla.dowsey@fife.gov.uk
URL: www.fifedirect.org.uk

INVERNESS-SHIRE

Highland Council Archive
Inverness Library
Farraline Park
Inverness
IV1 1NH
Tel: 01463 220 330
Fax: 01463 711 128

E-mail: archives@highland.gov.uk
URL: www.highland.gov.uk/leisure/
archives

KINCARDINESHIRE
See *Aberdeenshire, Aberdeenshire Council Archives*

KINROSS-SHIRE
Perth and Kinross Council Archive
A K Bell Library
York Place
Perth
PH2 8EP
Tel: 01738 477 012
Fax: 01738 477 010
E-mail: archives@pkc.gov.uk
URL:www.pkc.gov.uk/archives

KIRKCUDBRIGHTSHIRE
See *Dumfriesshire, Dumfries and Galloway Archives*

LANARKSHIRE
Glasgow City Council Archives and
Special Collections
The Mitchell
North Street
Glasgow
G3 7DN
Tel: 0141 287 2910
Fax: 0141 287 2815
E-mail: lil@cls.glasgow.gov.uk
URL: www.glasgow.gov.uk/en/
Residents/Leisure_Culture/Libraries/
Collections/FamilyHistory

MIDLOTHIAN
Midlothian Local Studies Centre
Midlothian District Library
2 Clerk Street
Loanhead
Midlothian
EH20 9DR
Tel: 0131 271 3976
Fax: 0131 440 4635

E-mail: local.studies@midlothian.gov.uk
URL: www.midlothian.gov.uk

MORAY
Elgin Library
Cooper Park
Elgin, Moray
IV30 1HS
Tel: 01343 562 644
Fax: 01343 562 630
E-mail: libstock@moray.gov.uk
URL: www.moray.org/index.html

NAIRNSHIRE
See *Inverness-shire, Highland Council Archive*

ORKNEY
Orkney Library and Archives
44 Junction Road
Kirkwall
KW15 1AG
Tel: 01856 873 166
Fax: 01856 875 260
E-mail: archives@orkneylibrary.org.uk
URL: www.orkneylibrary.org.uk

PEEBLESSHIRE
See *Berwickshire, Scottish Borders Archive and Local History Centre*

PERTHSHIRE
See *Kinross-shire, Perth* and *Kinross Library.*

Dundee City Archive & Record Centre
21 City Square
Dundee
DD1 3BY
Tel: 01382 434 494
Fax: 01382 434666
E-mail: archives@dundeecity.gov.uk
URL: www.dundeecity.gov.uk/archives

RENFREWSHIRE
Ross & Cromarty
See *Inverness-shire, Highland Council Archive*

Roxburghshire
See *Berwickshire, Scottish Borders Archive and Local History Centre*

Selkirkshire
See *Berwickshire, Scottish Borders Archive* and *Local History Centre*

SHETLAND
Shetland Archives
44 King Harald Street
Lerwick
ZE1 0EQ
Tel: 01595 696 247
Fax: 01595 696 533
E-mail: hetland.archives@sic.shetland.gov.uk
URL: www.shetland.gov.uk

STIRLINGSHIRE
Stirling Council Archives Services
5 Borrowmeadow Road
Stirling
FK7 7UW
Tel: 01786 450 745
E-mail: archive@stirling.gov.uk
URL: www.stirling.gov.uk

SUTHERLAND
See *Inverness-shire, Highland Council Archive*

WEST LOTHIAN
West Lothian Council Archives
9 Dunlop Square
Deans Industrial Estate
Livingston
West Lothian
EH54 8SB
Tel: 01506 773 770
E-mail: archive@westlothian.gov.uk
URL: www.westlothian.gov.uk/libraries

WIGTOWNSHIRE
See *Dumfriesshire, Dumfries and Galloway Archives*

WALES

THE NATIONAL LIBRARY OF WALES
Aberystwyth
Ceredigion
Wales
SY23 3BU
Tel: 01970 632 800
Fax: 01970 615 709
E-mail: holi@llgc.org.uk
URL: www.llgc.org.uk

COUNTY RECORD OFFICES AND OTHER ARCHIVES

ANGLESEY
Anglesey Record Office
Shire Hall
Glanhwfa Road
Llangefni
Anglesey
LL77 7TW
Tel: 01248 752 080
E-mail: archives@anglesey.gov.uk
URL: www.ynysmon.gov.uk/english/library/archives/archives.htm

BRECONSHIRE
Powys County Archives Office
County Hall
Llandrindod Wells
Powys
LD1 5LD
Tel: 1597 826 088
E-mail: archives@powys.gov.uk
URL: http://archives.powys.gov.uk

CAERNARFON
Caernarfon Record Office
Swyddfa'r Cyngor
Caernarfon
LL55 1SH
Tel: 01286 679 095
Fax: 01286 679 637
E-mail: archives.caernarfon@gwynedd.gov.uk

URL: www.gwynedd.gov.uk/gwy_doc.
asp?cat=3693&doc=12971

CARDIGAN
Ceredigion Archives
County Offices
Marine Terrace
Aberystwyth
Ceredigion
SY23 2DE
Tel: 01970 633 697 or 633 698
E-mail: archives@ceredigion.gov.uk
http://archifdy-ceredigion.org.uk

CARMARTHENSHIRE
Carmarthenshire Archives Service
Parc Myrddin
Richmond Terrace
Carmarthen
SA31 1DS
Tel: 01267 228 232
Fax: 01267 228 237
E-mail: archives@carmarthenshire.gov.uk
URL: www.carmarthenshire.gov.uk/
eng/index.asp?docID=6397

DENBIGH
Denbighshire Record Office
Ruthin Gaol
46 Clwyd Street
Ruthin
Denbighshire
LL15 1HP
Tel: 01824 708 250
E-mail: archives@denbighshire.gov.uk
URL: www.denbighshire.gov.uk/LL/
LifeLong.nsf/($All)/A3812426165ABD4
D80256FB7005391B8?OpenDocument

FLINTSHIRE
Flintshire Record Office
The Old Rectory
Hawarden
Flintshire
CH5 3NR.
Tel: 01244 532 364
Fax: 01244 538 344

E-mail: archives@flintshire.gov.uk
URL: www.flintshire.gov.uk/
webcont/newRealWeb.nsf/vwa_docref/
DEVS5RVL98

GLAMORGAN
Glamorgan Record Office
The Glamorgan Building
King Edward VII Avenue
Cathays Park
Cardiff
CF10 3NE
Telephone: 029 2078 0282
Fax: 029 2078 0284
E-mail: GlamRO@cardiff.ac.uk
URL: www.glamro.gov.uk

MERIONETH
Merionnydd Archives
Ffordd y Bala
Dolgellau
LL40 2YF
Tel: 01341 424 682
Fax: 01341 424 683
E-mail: archives.dolgellau@gwynedd.
gov.uk
URL: www.gwynedd.gov.uk/gwy_doc.
asp?cat=3265&doc=12971

MONMOUTHSHIRE
Gwent County Record Office
County Hall
Cwmbran
Gwent
NP44 2XH
Tel: 01633 644 886
E-mail: gwent.records@torfaen.gov.uk
URL: www.llgc.org.uk/cac/cac0004.
htm

MONTGOMERYSHIRE
Powys County Archives Office
County Hall
Llandrindod Wells
Powys
LD1 5LD
Tel: 01597 826 088

E-mail: archives@powys.gov.uk
URL: http://archives.powys.gov.uk

PEMBROKESHIRE
Pembrokeshire Record Office
The Castle
Haverfordwest
Pembrokeshire
SA61 2EF
Tel: 01437 763 707
Fax: 01437 768 539
URL: www.llgc.org.uk/cac/cac0002.
htm

RADNORSHIRE
Powys County Archives Office
County Hall
Llandrindod Wells
Powys
LD1 5LD
Tel: 01597 826 088
E-mail: archives@powys.gov.uk
URL: http://archives.powys.gov.uk

UNITED STATES

FAMILY HISTORY LIBRARY
35 North Temple Street
Salt Lake City, Utah
84150
USA
Tel: 801 240 2584
Fax: 801 240 1794
E-mail: fhl@ldsfs.net
URL: www.familysearch.org

To locate a Family History Center near
you, visit <www.familysearch.org/Eng/
Library/FHC/frameset_fhc.asp> and
enter a location.

Appendix C:
Questions Asked in Census
(1801–1901)

QUESTIONS ASKED IN CENSUSES OF ENGLAND, WALES, AND SCOTLAND, 1801–1901											
PERSONAL INFORMATION ON THE CENSUS	**1801**	**1811**	**1821**	**1831**	**1841**	**1851**	**1861**	**1871**	**1881**	**1891**	**1901**
Name (Given and Surname)					X	X	X	X	X	X	X
Sex	X	X	X	X	X	X	X	X	X	X	X
Age			X		X	X	X	X	X	X	X
Relationship to Head of Household						X	X	X	X	X	X
Marital Status						X	X	X	X	X	X
Birthplace					X	X	X	X	X	X	X
Nationality					X	X	X	X	X	X	X
Language Spoken (Gaelic\Welsh)*										X	X
Personal Occupation	X			X	X	X	X	X	X	X	X
Family Occupation		X	X	X							
Whether Employer					X	X	X	X	X	X	X
Whether Employed					X	X	X	X	X	X	X
Working on Own Account										X	X
At Home											X
Whether Unemployed								X	X		
Second Occupation						X	X	X	X	X	X
Attending School (Part or Full Time)‡						X	X	X	X	X	X
Receiving Regular Instruction at Home‡						X	X	X	X	X	X

PERSONAL INFORMATION ON THE CENSUS	1801	1811	1821	1831	1841	1851	1861	1871	1881	1891	1901
Religious Schedules						X					
Infirmity (deaf, dumb, blind, lunatic)						X	X	X	X	X	X
Number of baptisms, burials, marriages**	X	X	X	X	X						
Number of Inhabited Houses	X	X	X	X	X	X	X	X	X	X	X
Number of Families in Inhabited Houses	X	X	X	X							
Number of Houses Being Built		X	X	X	X	X	X	X	X	X	X
Number of Houses Uninhabited	X	X	X	X	X	X	X	X	X	X	X
Number of Rooms if Less Than Five										X	X
Rooms with One or More Windows†							X	X	X	X	X

* Asked only in Scotland and Wales

** Question not present for Scotland 1811–1841

† Scotland only

‡ 1881–1901 Scotland only

Appendix D: Population

CENSUS YEAR	ENGLAND AND WALES	SCOTLAND
1841	15,914,148	2,620,184
1851	17,927,609	2,888,742
1861	20,066,224	3,062,294
1871	22,712,266	3,360,018
1881	25,974,439	3,735,573
1891	29,002,525	4,025,647
1901	32,527,843	4,472,103

Appendix E: Worksheets

On the following pages, you will find blank census forms for England from 1841 through 1901 and for Scotland in 1841. They can help you decipher poor images and keep track of information.

1841 Census Form

For more family history charts and forms, visit
http://www.ancestry.co.uk/save/charts/census.htm

Country: _____ H.O./ _____ Book: _____ Folio: _____ Page: _____ E.D.: _____

| PLACE | HOUSES | | NAMES of each Person who abode therein the preceeding Night. | AGE and SEX | | PROFESSION, TRADE, EMPLOYMENT, or of INDEPENDENT MEANS. | Where Born | |
	Uninhabited or Building	Inhabited		Males	Females		Whether Born in same County	Whether Born in Scotland, Ireland, or Foreign Parts.
TOTAL in Page ____								

1841 Scotland Census Form

Parish of: _____

For more family history charts and forms, visit
http://www.ancestry.co.uk/save/charts/census.htm

1			2			3	4	
PLACE	HOUSES		NAME and SURNAME, SEX and AGE, of each Person who abode in each House on the Night of 6th June.			OCCUPATION	Where Born	
Here insert Name of Village, Street, Square, Close, Court, &c.	Uninhabited or Building	Inhabited	NAME and SURNAME	AGE		Of what Profession, Trade, Employment, or whether of Independent Means.	If Born in Scotland, state Whether in County or otherwise.	Whether Foreign-er, or whether Born in England or Ireland.
				Male	Female			
TOTAL in Page ____								

1851 Census Form

Country: _____

Piece #: H.O./ _____

Folio: _____

Page: _____

Enumeration District: _____

The undermentioned Houses are situate within the Boundaries of the

Parish or Township of	Ecclesiastical District of	City or Borough of	Town of	Villiage of

No. of House-holder's Schedule	Name of Street, Place, or Road, and Name or No. of House	Name and Surname of each Person who abode in the house, on the Night of the 30th March, 1851	Relation to Head of Family	Condition	Age of Males	Age of Females	Rank, Profession, or Occupation	Where Born	Whether Blind, or Deaf and-Dumb

Total of Houses

Total of Persons...

I _____ U _____ B _____

1861 Census Form

Country: _____

Piece #: RG 9/ _____

Folio: _____

Page: _____

Enumeration District: _____

The undermentioned Houses are situate within the Boundaries of the

Parish [or Township] of	City or Municipal Borough of	Municipal Ward of	Parliamentary Borough of	Town of	Hamlet or Tything, &c., of	Ecclesiastical District of

No. of Schedule	Road, Street, &c., and No. or Name of House	HOUSES		Name and Surname of each Person	Relation to Head of Family	Condition	Age of		Rank, Profession, or Occupation	Where Born	Whether Blind, or Deaf and-Dumb
		In-habited	Unin-habited (U.), or Building (B.)				Males	Females			
Total of Houses...							Total of Males and Females...				

1871 Census Form

For more family history charts and forms, visit
http://www.ancestry.co.uk/save/charts/census.htm

Country: _____

Piece #: RG10/ _____

Folio: _____

Page: _____

Enumeration District: _____

The undermentioned Houses are situate within the Boundaries of the

Civil Parish [or Township] of	City or Municipal Borough of	Municipal Ward of	Parlimentary Borough of	Town of	Villiage or Hamlet, &c., of	Local Board, or [Improvement Commisioners District] of	Ecclesiastical District of

No of Schedule	ROAD, STREET, &c., and No. or NAME of HOUSE	HOUSES		NAME and Surname of each Person	RELATION to Head of Family	CON-DITION	AGE of		Rank, profession, or OCCUPATION	WHERE BORN	Whether (1) Deaf-and-Dumb (2) Blind (3) Imbecile or Idiot (4) Lunatic
		In-habited	Unin-habited (U.), or Building (B.)				Males	Females			

Total of Houses...

Total of Males and Females...

NOTE—*Draw your pen through such words of the headings as are inapplicable.*

1881 Census Form

Country: _____ Piece #: RG11/_____ Folio: _____ Page: _____ Enumeration District: _____

The undermentioned Houses are situate within the Boundaries of the

Civil Parish [or Township] of	City or Municipal Borough of	Municipal Ward of	Parlimentary Borough of	Town or Villiage or Hamlet of	Urban Sanitary District of	Rural Sanitary District of	Ecclesiastical Parish or District of

No. of Schedule	ROAD, STREET, &c., and No. or NAME of HOUSE	HOUSES		NAME and Surname of each Person	RELATION to Head of Family	CON-DITION as to Marriage	AGE last Birthday of		Rank, profession, or OCCUPATION	WHERE BORN	If (1) Deaf-and-Dumb (2) Blinda (3) Imbecile or Idiot (4) Lunatic
		In-habited	Unin-habited (U.) or Building (B.)				Males	Females			

Total of Houses...   Total of Males and Females...

NOTE—*Draw your pen through such words of the headings as are inapplicable.*

1891 Census Form

Country: _____ Piece #: RG12/ _____ Folio: _____ Page: _____ Enumeration District: _____

Administrative County of _____

The Undermentioned Houses are situate within the Boundaries of the

Civil Parish	Municipal Borough	Municipal Ward	Urban Sanitary District	Town or Village or Hamlet	Rural Sanitary District	Parliamentary Borough or Division	Ecclesiastical Parish or District
of ___	of ___	of ___	of ___	of ___	of ___	of ___	of ___

Cols. 1	2	3	4	5	6	7	8	9	10	11	12	13	14	15	16
No. of Schedule	ROAD, STREET, &c., and No. or NAME of HOUSE	HOUSES In-habit-ed	Unin-habited (U.), or Building (B.)	Number of rooms occupied if less than five	NAME and Surname of each Person	RELATION to Head of Family	CON-DITION as to Marriage	AGE last Birthday of — Males	Females	PROFESSION or OCCUPATION	Employer	Employed	Neither Employer nor Employed	WHERE BORN	If (1) Deaf-and-Dumb (2) Blind (3) Lunatic, Imbecile, or Idiot

Total of Houses and of Tenements with less than Five Rooms…

Total of Males and Females…

(The next Schedule to be entered on the following page).

NOTE—*Draw the pen through such of the words of the headings as are inappropriate*

1901 Census Form

Country: _____   Piece #: RG13/ _____   Folio: _____   Page: _____   Enumeration District: _____

Administrative County _____

The undermentioned Houses are situate within the boundaries of the

| Civil Parish of _____ | Ecclesiastical Parish of _____ | County Borough, Municipal Borough, or Urban District of _____ | Ward of Municipal Borough or of Urban district of _____ | Rural District of _____ | Parlimentary Borough or Division of _____ | Town or Villiage or Hamlet of _____ |

Cols 1	2	3	4	5	6	7	8	9	10	11	12	13	14	15	16	17
			HOUSES							Age last Birthday of						If
No of Schedule	ROAD, STREET, &c., and No. or NAME of HOUSE	In-habited	Uninhabited — In Occupa-tion	Uninhabited — Not in Occupa-tion	Building	Number of Rooms occupied if less than five	Name and Surname of each Person	RELATION to Head of Family	Condition as to Marriage	Males	Females	PROFESSION OR OCCUPATION	Employer, Worker, or Own account	If Working at Home	WHERE BORN	(1) Deaf and Dumb (2) Blind (3) Lunatic (4) Imbecile, feeble-minded

Total of Schedules of Houses and of Tene-ments with less than Five Rooms {   Total of Males and Females...

NOTE—*Draw your pen through such words of the headings as are inapplicable.*

Appendix F: Missing Returns

ENGLAND, WALES, CHANNEL ISLAND, ISLE OF MAN		
PARISHES LISTED AS MISSING IN THE TNA CATALOG		
1891		
PIECE	**COUNTY**	**PARISH MISSING IN WHOLE OR PART**
RG 12/64	London	Chelsea
RG 12/217	London	St Clement Danes
RG 12/292	London	Ratcliff
RG 12/636	Kent	Crayford
RG 12/637	Kent	Crayford
RG 12/638	Kent	Crayford
RG 12/656	Kent	Rochester
RG 12/657	Kent	Rochester
RG 12/658	Kent	Rochester
RG 12/667	Kent	Gillingham
RG 12/710	Kent	Herne
RG 12/711	Kent	Seasalter
RG 12/885	Hampshire	Northwood
RG 12/886	Hampshire	Northwood and Whippingham
RG 12/1042	Middlesex	Willesden
RG 12/1043	Middlesex	Willesden
RG 12/1145	Buckinghamshire	Aylesbury
RG 12/1340	Essex	East Ham
RG 12/1341	Essex	East Ham
RG 12/1731	Devon	St Andrew, Plymouth
RG 12/1732	Devon	St Andrew, Plymouth
RG 12/1733	Devon	St Andrew, Plymouth
RG 12/1734	Devon	St Andrew, Plymouth
RG 12/1735	Devon	St Andrew, Plymouth

RG 12/1746	Devon	Stoke Damerel
RG 12/1747	Devon	Stoke Damerel
RG 12/2168	Staffordshire	Stoke upon Trent
RG 12/2247	Staffordshire	Walsall Foreign
RG 12/2486	Warwickshire	Compton Wyniates
RG 12/2538	Leicestershire	St Mary, Leicester
RG 12/2614	Lincolnshire	Great Grimsby
RG 12/2615	Lincolnshire	Great Grimsby
RG 12/2616	Lincolnshire	Great Grimsby
RG 12/2619	Lincolnshire	Clee with Weelsby
RG 12/2719	Lincolnshire	Kegworth
RG 12/2736	Derbyshire	St Alkmund
RG 12/2737	Derbyshire	St Alkmund
RG 12/2738	Derbyshire	St Alkmund
RG 12/2831	Cheshire	Runcorn
RG 12/2832	Cheshire	Runcorn
RG 12/2833	Cheshire	Weston
RG 12/2878	Cheshire	Birkenhead
RG 12/2898	Lancashire	Liverpool
RG 12/2969	Lancashire	Bootle cum Linacre
RG 12/2970	Lancashire	Bootle cum Linacre
RG 12/3872	Yorkshire	Goole
RG 12/3873	Yorkshire	Goole
RG 12/3922	Yorkshire	Drypool
RG 12/3923	Yorkshire	Southcoates
RG 12/3924	Yorkshire	Southcoates
RG 12/3925	Yorkshire	Southcoates
RG 12/3925	Yorkshire	Garrison Side
RG 12/3936	Yorkshire	Holy Trinity and St Mary
RG 12/4004	Yorkshire	Middlesbrough
RG 12/4011	Yorkshire	Linthorpe
RG 12/4058	Durham	Throston
RG 12/4059	Durham	Hartlepool
RG 12/4061	Durham	Stranton
RG 12/4170	Durham	Hedworth, Monkton and Yarrow
RG 12/4364	Monmouthshire	Mamhilad
RG 12/4385	Glamorgan	Roath
RG 12/4397	Glamorgan	St Mary, Cardiff
RG 12/4555	Cardiganshire	Llanllwchaiarn

1871		
PIECE	**COUNTY**	**PARISH MISSING IN WHOLE OR PART**
RG 10/3278	Leicestershire	St Margaret, Leicester
RG 10/4729	Yorkshire	Eastoft and Haldenby
RG 10/5444	Glamorgan	Llangyfelach, Penderry, and Llandilotalybont

| RG 10/5590 | Breconshire | Talgarth, Grwyne-fawr and Grwyne-fechan |
| RG 10/4213 | Lancashire | Preston |

1861

PIECE	COUNTY	PARISH MISSING IN WHOLE OR PART
RG 9/219	Middlesex	St Dunstan-in-the-West
RG 9/485	Kent	Wateringbury
RG 9/541	Kent	Goodnestone
RG 9/1047	Cambridgeshire	Leverington
RG 9/1194	Norfolk	Great Yarmouth
RG 9/3652	Yorkshire	Marske
RG 9/3735	Durham	Brancepeth
RG 9/3855	Northumberland	Newburn
RG 9/4014	Monmouthshire	Llangattock
RG 9/4014	Monmouthshire	Magor
RG 9/4024	Glamorgan	Michaelstoneyvedw
RG 9/4027	Glamorgan	Machen
RG 9/4079	Glamorgan	Tythegston
RG 9/4187	Carmarthenshire	Llanycrwys
RG 9/4211	Breconshire	St David, Brecon
RG 9/4225	Breconshire	Llanigon and Hay
RG 9/4228	Radnorshire	Radnor
RG 9/4261	Montgomeryshire	Llansaintffraid
RG 9/4262	Montgomeryshire	Guilsfield
RG 9/4263	Montgomeryshire	Guilsfield and Llanfyllin
RG 9/4265	Denbighshire	Llanarmonmynyddmawr
RG 9/4276	Flintshire	Mold
RG 9/4309	Merionethshire	Llanfihangel-glynmyfyr
RG 9/4389	Guernsey	Island of Sark

1851

PIECE	COUNTY	PARISH MISSING IN WHOLE OR PART
HO 107/1762	Cambridgeshire	Newmarket, Snailwell, Landwade, Burwell, Swaffham Prior and Ashley-cum-Silverley
HO 107/1762	Suffolk	St Mary and Exning
HO 107/1763	Cambridgeshire	Kennett
HO 107/1763	Suffolk	Lidgate, Ousden, Dalham, Gazeley and Moulton
HO 107/1785	Essex	Felstead, Stebbing, Bardfield-Saling, Great Bardfield, Lindsell, Little Easton, Great Dunmow, Little Dunmow, Barnston, Great Canfield, Little Canfield, Takeley, Hatfield Broad Oak or Hatfield Regis, White Roothing, Aythorpe Roothing, Leaden Roothing, Margaret Roothing, High Easter, High Roothing, Great Easton, Tilty, Broxted, Chickney, Thaxted and Little Bardfield

HO 107/1852	Dorset	Sturminster Newton Castle, Hinton St Mary, Manston, Hammoon, Child Okeford, Shillingstone, Okeford Fitzpaine, Fifehead Neville, Haselbury Bryan, Stoke Wake, Woolland, Ibberton and Bellchalwell

1841		
PIECE	**COUNTY**	**PARISH MISSING IN WHOLE OR PART**
HO 107/89	Cheshire	Malpas, Shocklach and Threapwood
HO 107/192	Derbyshire	Walton-upon-Trent
HO 107/404	Southampshire	Winnall
HO 107/465	Kent	Bishopsbourne
HO 107/467	Kent	Herne Bay
HO 107/469	Kent	Reculver
HO 107/470	Kent	Sturry, Swalecliffe, Westbere, Seasalter Liberty and Whitstable
HO 107/471	Kent	Ashford
HO 107/475	Kent	Smarden
HO 107/668	Middlesex	St Luke
HO 107/680	Middlesex	Paddington
HO 107/690	Middlesex	Kensington
HO 107/797	Northamptonshire	Blatherwycke, Bulwick, Bulwick Short Leys, Deene and Great Weldon
HO 107/798	Northamptonshire	Weedon-Beck
HO 107/809	Northamptonshire	Haselbeech
HO 107/890	Oxfordshire	Yarnton
HO 107/942	Somerset	Mells
HO 107/1071	Surrey	Walton-upon-Thames and Weybridge
HO 107/1075	Surrey	Malden
HO 107/1172	Wiltshire	Hardenhuish
HO 107/1174	Wiltshire	Downton and No Man's Land
HO 107/1176	Wiltshire	Patney
HO 107/1184	Wiltshire	Bishop's Cannings and West Lavington
HO 107/1186	Wiltshire	Allcannings, Alton Barnes, Beeching Stoke, Chirton, Market Lavington, Marden, St Bernard Stanton and Urchfont
HO 107/1286	Yorkshire	Ripon
HO 107/1369	Breconshire	Llanhamlach and Vainor
HO 107/1404	Denbighshire	Clocaenog, Derwen, Llanelidan and Llanfair Dyffrin Clwyd
HO 107/1405	Denbighshire	Llanaron
HO 107/1408	Flintshire	Bangor, Erbistock, Hope, Llanarmon, Threapwood, Worthenbury, Wrexham and Malpas
HO 107/1409	Flintshire	Gresford
HO 107/1410	Flintshire	Mold
HO 107/1415	Glamorganshire	Merthyr-Tydfil
HO 107/1416	Glamorganshire	Cowbridge and Llan-blethian
HO 107/1423	Glamorganshire	St Bride Major

SCOTLAND		
1881		
DISTRICT\ PARISH NUMBER	**COUNTY**	**PARISH MISSING IN WHOLE OR PART**
821	Dumfriesshire	Dumfries
822	Dumfriesshire	Dunscore
1841		
DISTRICT\ PARISH NUMBER	**COUNTY**	**PARISH MISSING IN WHOLE OR PART**
93	Moray	Cromdale
167	Banffshire	Seafield
324	Perthshire	Aberfeldy
367	Perthshire	Kinloch Rannoch
400	Fifeshire	Abdie
406	Fifeshire	Auchtermuchty
409	Fifeshire	Balmerino
415	Fifeshire	Ceres
416	Fifeshire	Collesie
418	Fifeshire	Creich
419	Fifeshire	Cults
420	Fifeshire	Cupar
421	Fifeshire	Dairsie
423	Fifeshire	Dunbog
439	Fifeshire	Kinghorn
440	Fifeshire	Kinglasie
442	Fifeshire	Kirkcaldy
444	Fifeshire	Leslie
509	Argyllshire	Cumlodden
535	Argyllshire	Tarbert
556	Buteshire	Lochranza
557	Buteshire	NorthBute
577	Ayshire	Auchinleck
776	Selkirkshire	Kirkhope
809	Roxburghshire	Teviothead
862	Kirkcudbrightshire	CorsockBridge
864	Kirkcudbrightshire	Dalbeattie

Bibliography

————. *Population Tables I: Numbers of Inhabitants: 1852–53* (1631–1632), LXXXV, 1.

————. *Population Tables I: Numbers and Distribution of the People: 1862* (3056), L, 1.

————. *Population Tables: Area, Houses and Inhabitants, Counties: 1872* (C. 676), LXVI, Pt I, 1; *Vol II, Registration or Union Counties*: 1872 (C.676–I), LXVI, Pt II, 1.

————. *Population Tables: Area, Houses and Population: Counties: 1883* (C. 3562), LXXVIII, 1.

————. *Population Tables: Area, Houses and Population: Counties: 1893–94* (C.6948), CIV, 1.

————. *Summary Tables: Areas, Houses and Population: 1903* (Cd 1523), LXXXIV, 1.

Chapman, Colin R. *Pre-1841 Censuses and Population Listings in the British Isles.* 5th ed. Dursley, England: Lockin Publishing, 1998.

Gibson, Jeremy. *Marriage, Census and Other Indexes for Family Historians.* 8th ed. Birmingham: Federation of Family History Societies, 2000.

Gibson, Jeremy, and Elizabeth Hampson. "Census Returns, 1841–1891." In *Microform: A Directory to Local Holdings in Great Britain; Channel Islands; Isle of Man.* 6th ed. Birmingham: Federation of Family History Societies, 1994.

Gibson, Jeremy, and M. Medlycott. *Local Census Listings 1522–1930, Holdings in the British Isles.* 3rd ed. Birmingham: Federation of Family History Societies, 1997.

Great Britain. House of Commons. *Statements on Population: 1841,* sess. II, (52), II, 277.

Herber, Mark D. *Ancestral Trails: The Complete Guide to British Genealogy and Family History*. Baltimore, Md.: Genealogical Publishing Co., 1998.

Higgs, Edward J. *Making Sense of the Census: The Manuscript Returns for England and Wales, 1801–1901*. London: Her Majesty's Stationary Office, 1989.

————. *A Clearer Sense of the Census*. London: Her Majesty's Stationary Office, 1996.

Humphrey-Smith, Cecil, ed. *The Phillimore Atlas and Index of Parish Registers*. 3rd ed. Chichester, England: Phillimore, 2003.

Index of Place Names Showing the Library Microfilm Numbers for the 1841–1891 Census of England, Wales, Isle of Man, and Channel Islands. Salt Lake City: Family History Library, 1992.

Johnson, Gordon. *Census Records for Scottish Families at Home and Abroad*. 3rd ed. Aberdeen: Aberdeen and North East Scotland Family History Society, 1997.

Jonas, Linda, and Paul Milner. *A Genealogist's Guide to Discovering Your Scottish Ancestors*. Cincinnati: Betterway Books, 2002.

Lumas, Susan. *Making Use of the Census*. 4th ed. London: Public Records Office Publications, 2002.

McLaughlin, Eve. *The Censuses, 1841–1881, Use and Interpretation*. 3rd ed. Mclaughlin Guide Series. Solihull, West Midlands: Federation of Family History Societies, 1985.

Metropolitan Board of Works. *Names of Streets and Places within the Metropolitan Area: As Defined by the Local Management Act, 1855, Shewing Postal Districts, Localities and Parishes and Appendix of Names Adopted during the Progress of This Work*. London: Superintending Architect's Dept., 1887.

Office of Population Censuses and Surveys. *Report on 1851 Census, Great Britain: Including Population Tables, 1801–1851*. London: Her Majesty's Stationary Office, 1852.

————. *Guide to Census Reports, Great Britain, 1808–1966*. London: Her Majesty's Stationary Office, 1977.

————. *Census 1981 Historical Tables, 1801–1981, England and Wales*. London: Her Majesty's Stationary Office, 1982.

Ouimette, David S. *Finding Your Irish Ancestors: A Beginner's Guide*. Provo, Utah: Ancestry, 2005.

People and Places in the Victorian Census: A Review and Bibliography of Publications Based Substantially on the Manuscript Census Enumerators' Books, 1841–1911. London:

W. Clowes and Sons for Her Majesty's Stationary Office, 1852. Reprint, Historical Geography Research Series, no. 23. Cambridge, England: Cambridge Group for the History of Population and Social Structure, 1989.

Public Records Office. *Using Census Returns.* Pocket Guides to PRO. Richmond, Surrey: Public Record Office, 2000.

Rosier, Margaret E. Bryant. *Index to Census Registration Districts.* 6th ed. Federation of Family History Societies, 1999.

Ruthven-Murray, Peter. *Scottish Census Indexes: Covering the 1841–1871 Civil Censuses.* 3rd ed. Scotland: Scottish Association of Family History Societies, 1998.

Sinclair, Cecil. *Jock Tamson's Bairns: A History of the Records of the General Register Office for Scotland.* Edinburgh: General Register Office for Scotland, 2000.

Withycombe, Elizabeth Gidley. *The Oxford Dictionary of English Christian Names.* 3rd ed. Oxford, England: New York: Clarendon, 1977.

Index

About the Author

Echo King, AG graduated from Brigham Young University with a degree in Family History. She specializes in English research. Echo currently serves as the ICAPGEN Renewal Secretary and has worked for Ancestry.com in the Digital Preservation Department for more than six years.

Printed in the USA
CPSIA information can be obtained
at www.ICGtesting.com
JSHW060046150824
68134JS00031B/2654

9 781593 313005